A British Childhood? Some Historical Reflections on Continuities and Discontinuities in the Culture of Anglophone Childhood

A British Childhood? Some Historical Reflections on Continuities and Discontinuities in the Culture of Anglophone Childhood

Special Issue Editor
Pam Jarvis

MDPI • Basel • Beijing • Wuhan • Barcelona • Belgrade

Special Issue Editor
Pam Jarvis
Leeds Trinity University
UK

Editorial Office
MDPI
St. Alban-Anlage 66
4052 Basel, Switzerland

This is a reprint of articles from the Special Issue published online in the open access journal *Genealogy* (ISSN 2313-5778) in 2019 (available at: https://www.mdpi.com/journal/genealogy/special_issues/britishchildhood).

For citation purposes, cite each article independently as indicated on the article page online and as indicated below:

LastName, A.A.; LastName, B.B.; LastName, C.C. Article Title. *Journal Name* **Year**, *Article Number*, Page Range.

ISBN 978-3-03921-934-6 (Pbk)
ISBN 978-3-03921-935-3 (PDF)

Cover image courtesy of Pam Jarvis.

© 2019 by the authors. Articles in this book are Open Access and distributed under the Creative Commons Attribution (CC BY) license, which allows users to download, copy and build upon published articles, as long as the author and publisher are properly credited, which ensures maximum dissemination and a wider impact of our publications.
The book as a whole is distributed by MDPI under the terms and conditions of the Creative Commons license CC BY-NC-ND.

Contents

About the Special Issue Editor vii

Preface to "A British Childhood? Some Historical Reflections on Continuities and
Discontinuities in the Culture of Anglophone Childhood" ix

Pam Jarvis
Not Just 'Once' upon a Time
Reprinted from: *Genealogy* **2019**, *3*, 44, doi:10.3390/genealogy3030044 1

Mark Malisa and Thelma Quardey Missedja
Schooled for Servitude: The Education of African Children in British Colonies, 1910–1990
Reprinted from: *Genealogy* **2019**, *3*, 40, doi:10.3390/genealogy3030040 15

Yinka Olusoga
Younger Infants in the Elementary School: Discursively Constructing the Under-Fives in
Institutional Spaces and Practices
Reprinted from: *Genealogy* **2019**, *3*, 37, doi:10.3390/genealogy3030037 27

Betty Liebovich
Margaret McMillan's Contributions to Cultures of Childhood
Reprinted from: *Genealogy* **2019**, *3*, 43, doi:10.3390/genealogy3030043 45

Philip Hood
Does Early Childhood Education in England for the 2020s Need to Rediscover Susan Isaacs:
Child of the Late Victorian Age and Pioneering Educational Thinker?
Reprinted from: *Genealogy* **2019**, *3*, 39, doi:10.3390/genealogy3030039 58

Claire Phillips
Child Abandonment in England, 1741–1834: The Case of the London Foundling Hospital
Reprinted from: *Genealogy* **2019**, *3*, 35, doi:10.3390/genealogy3030035 69

About the Special Issue Editor

Pam Jarvis is a Chartered Psychologist (British Psychological Society) and qualified teacher with additional academic qualifications in history and education. She works within a multidisciplinary research perspective, considering psychological, biological, social, and historical perspectives of childhood. Her PhD research focused upon play-based learning in 4–6 year olds. She has published extensively as an academic author, including serving as Editor of the book 'Perspectives on Play', which has been published in three successive English editions, and additionally in Greek and Portuguese (Brazil). The key focus of her research and writing is on the wellbeing of children, young people, and their families, as well as the development of social policies to support them. She is currently an Honorary Research Fellow of the Institute of Childhood and Education at Leeds Trinity University.

Preface to "A British Childhood? Some Historical Reflections on Continuities and Discontinuities in the Culture of Anglophone Childhood"

This book considers the history of childhood through a focus upon continuities and discontinuities in British and affiliated Anglophone cultures. It begins with Not Just 'Once' upon a Time by Pam Jarvis, a reflection upon the changing nature of Western childhood, focusing upon traces that previous generations have left in 'folk' and 'fairy' tales and rhymes. Such tales and their underpinning narratives were further disseminated across the world via British colonial culture, and currently play a large role in contemporary US multimedia products; the implications of this process are considered. The role of psychobiological and evolutionary factors in human storytelling provides an underpinning theoretical basis for this article. Mark Malisa and Thelma Quardey Missedja pick up upon the dissemination of British culture through colonisation in their article Schooled for Servitude: The Education of African Children in British Colonies, 1910–1990, pointing out that the invaders did not introduce education into their African colonies as is frequently claimed, but instead changed and channelised it so that it carried messages of conquest and colonialism. Yinka Olusoga describes a similar process of conditioning undertaken with the working classes in England in her article Younger Infants in the Elementary School: Discursively Constructing the Under-Fives in Institutional Spaces and Practices, reflecting upon how young children were reconstructed as 'scholars' by Victorian industrialists. In Margaret McMillan's Contributions to Cultures of Childhood, Betty Liebovich considers a positive early twentieth century development upon this bleak, functional construction of the working-class child, exploring the work of Christian Socialists Margaret and Rachel McMillan with working-class children in London. These sisters developed a holistic pedagogy which encompassed both education and care, preparing the ground for the modern British nursery school. In their chapter Does Early Childhood Education in England for the 2020s Need to Rediscover Susan Isaacs: Child of the Late Victorian Age and Pioneering Educational Thinker, Philip Hood and Kristina Tobutt question whether 21st century Britain might have much to learn from the style of practice pioneered by the McMillans, in particular, moving away from narrow 'information transmission' practice in contemporary education and subsequently embracing a more holistic approach to child learning and development. They illustrate their chapter with ideas drawn from the practice of Susan Isaacs in her 1930s experimental nursery school. Finally, in her chapter Child Abandonment in England, 1743–1834: The Case of the London Foundling Hospital, Claire Phillips considers the dawning of the modern conception of vulnerable childhood, documenting the increasingly conscious recognition of children's particular developmental needs over the late eighteenth and early nineteenth century. She focuses upon the diligent work that 'Foundling Hospitals' undertook to nurture and protect young children who had been abandoned by their parents. Overall, the articles consider a range of perspectives upon how parents and teachers attempt to socialise young children into the adults that it aspires to produce at the relevant time, and the impacts of wider society upon this process.

Pam Jarvis
Special Issue Editor

Review
Not Just 'Once' upon a Time

Pam Jarvis

Institute of Childhood and Education, Leeds Trinity University, Horsforth, Leeds LS18 5HD, UK; p.jarvis@leedstrinity.ac.uk

Received: 30 April 2019; Accepted: 31 July 2019; Published: 1 August 2019

Abstract: Multidisciplinary research indicates the importance of storytelling in child development, most recently exploring the evolved nature of language and narrative. Many questions remain about how children develop competence within such a vital but highly complex process. The 'once upon a time' concept is present within nearly every human language on Earth, indicating what a powerful hold 'storying' has over human beings and what a central role it plays within human societies. Sue Lyle proposes that human beings are above all, 'storytelling animals'. Emergent questions include whether and how current mass-produced storytelling products and interactive media developed by Western technology impact children's competence in the human 'storying' process and, in particular, whether such rapid change should be approached with more reflection and caution than is currently the case. In this article, I will consider the process of child development with respect to language and 'storying', the traditional role of stories and 'make-believe' in the fabric of children's lives, how this has changed in the recent past in technologically advancing societies, and how such change may impact children's learning and development.

Keywords: narrative; storying; mythology; human evolution; children; play; media

1. What Do We Know about Language, Narrative, and Evolution?

The role of language and culture creates a crucial separation, distinguishing human from non-human animals (Bruner 1976, 1990, 1996; Bronfenbrenner and Ceci 1994; Low 1989; Tomasello 1999; Geary 1998; Dunbar et al. 1999; Boyd 2009, 2018) and underpinning greater environmentally mediated plasticity within human beings. Thus, language and culture bestow on humans a huge capacity to individually understand and innovatively adapt to different environments.

Jerome Bruner proposed that human beings are creatures who evolved to critically rely upon sharing symbolic meaning to operate within their world, 'depending upon the human capacity to internalise language and use its system of signs ... such a social meaning readiness is a product of our evolutionary past' (Bruner 1990, p. 69). He later reflected on the way that human beings understand many, sometimes deceptively similar, aspects of their world very differently, depending on the meanings that they attach to them (Bruner 1996):

> Humans can do [what] other primate species cannot do. We organise social systems, networks of interaction that require cooperation between individuals who may never have seen one another before and who may never expect to see one another again. (Chase 1999, p. 36)

Bruner (1991, p. 9) emphasized the central role that narrative comprehension plays in this process, proposing that it is 'among the earliest powers of mind to appear in the young child and among the most widely used forms of organizing human experience'. Lyle (2000) agreed, describing human beings as a storying animal, making sense of thoughts and events via stories and narratives, with the result that human beings live in 'a largely story shaped world' (Lyle 2000, p. 55).

This is an essentially 'biocultural' paradigm (e.g., Tomasello 1999; Bruner 1996; Jarvis 2006) in which the evolved human competency for symbolic communication is mediated through language, which shapes and gives meaning to individual human lives and thence to human societies. The human primate comes equipped with the potential for enormous elasticity in cognitive and social development, far outreaching any other species on Earth, underpinned by this ability to reason and communicate through abstract symbolic thought, which is principally rooted in language. There is an important 'priming' role for biology in providing a template for human development, in partnership with a huge amount of plasticity, to allow a person to shape him/herself to the environment in which he/she develops. With increasing maturity, human beings additionally become the only creatures on Earth with the ability to flexibly adjust themselves to different environments via the use of manufactured equipment and, to some extent, the environments themselves.

While the biocultural model of the human being has recently generated a significant amount of debate between psychologists, philosophers, biologists, and anthropologists, human fascination with their own capacity for language, storytelling, and narrative are much older. The ancient Greek philosophers Plato and Aristotle discussed the distinction between deeply rooted narrative forms within human cognition and how these gave rise to a range of specific stories (Swearingen 1990). The 'story' refers to a specific sequence of events in which certain characters and situations appear (for example, Cinderella, the ball, and the slipper or Snow White, the mirror, and the enchanted sleep); the 'narrative' is the underlying cultural message that 'lies beneath' (for example, the beautiful, oppressed princess, the wicked stepmother, and the handsome savior prince).

In this article, I will focus upon a very small corner of this arena: the issue of storytelling in childhood and its perceived function, history, and future potential. I will rely upon a theoretical concept of the human being as a biocultural creature, involving 'a confluence between innate and learned influences' (Mallon and Stich 2000, p. 143). The issues addressed will be premised upon on Tinbergen (1963) questions relating to development, function, and history (Wilson 2019), and through this lens, the role of 'storying' during the human developmental period will be explored, as well as how modes of storying have recently changed in Western culture in tandem with technological advancement. First of all, I will investigate how children develop an understanding of how to engage with human 'storying' and begin to create storying activities of their own, and then, I will subsequently explore some examples of storying in a range of cultures. Particular attention will be paid to how storying has recently changed within the technologically advancing environment of the English-speaking West and some consequent potential impacts upon contemporary Western early childhood.

2. How Do Children Develop the Capacity to 'Story'?

It has long been observed that parents engage with their infants in 'protoconversations' (Bateson 1975), in which the turn-taking elements of speech can be discerned—the child and the adult vocalizing in turn. Most recently, Yoo et al. (2018) discovered that caregivers engage in this type of behavior in response to babies' 'protophones' (early speech-like noises, such as coos and gurgles) but not in response to cries, indicating a natural human awareness of the functional difference between the noises that babies make. Zeedyk (2006, p. 322) describes the early protoconversation interactions of babies and caregivers as a rhythmic 'jazz duet', in which the baby and the adult exchange expressions, noises, and eye contact in a type of improvised symbolic 'dance'. This is not always led by the adult; the baby quickly becomes an equal partner in signaling the beginning, end, and direction of the 'dance'. The adult helps the infant to learn to 'story' such interactions through their contributions, initially in very simple games, such as peek-a-boo—"here I am ... I've gone again"—and a little later in infancy in more sophisticated play episodes, for example, "what are you doing with teddy, giving him a cuddle? Shall we sing to him ... ".

In non-literate societies, as linguistic competence increases, children are introduced to the stories and myths of their culture by adults; for example, this is the role of grandparents within traditional Native Australian society (Ungunmerr-Baumann 1988). Most contemporary Western parents read to their children from a very early point in life and are strongly encouraged to do so within their cultural milieu, through government-produced advice to parents and charity-funded initiatives. For example, the United States (US)/United Kingdom (UK) charity 'Imagination Library' provides one free book a month to children under the age of five registered with their website. Through this progressive regime of introduction to language, narrative, and storying during early childhood, human beings are inducted into the overarching narratives of human existence that societies craft into culturally relevant 'storying'. Jung (2003) referred to the characters and events that inhabit such grand narratives as 'archetypes' that commonly appear in myths and fairy tales, for example, the beautiful young woman in need of rescue, the young man on a journey who becomes the rescuer and hence the hero, the wise old man who acts as a mentor to the young man, and the wicked witch who becomes the antagonist. As demonstrated by well-known Western fairy tales, such as Cinderella, Sleeping Beauty, and Snow White, the same narrative can underpin a number of different stories. 'The archetype is essentially an unconscious content that is altered by becoming conscious and by being perceived, and it takes its color from the individual consciousness in which it happens to appear' (Jung 2003, p. 4).

This inherent level of flexibility, in which culture plays a crucial role in the process of weaving a story around a narrative, indicates the complex interaction of the biological and the cultural within the human being. When we engage with a story, we do so through a cultural filter rather than by simply absorbing basic content, and while that filter will, in turn, play an important role in the re-telling, the story is never entirely fixed by it. In a commentary on the philosopher E. D. Hirsch's concept of 'validity in interpretation' (Hirsch 1967), Michael McGuire comments:

> I break from Hirsch ... not only the author's intentions constitute an epistemic structure of a narrative against which interpretations can be measured, but the participation of a narrative in a language of earlier texts and thoughts is necessary to the interpretation of that particular narrative. (McGuire 1990, p. 229)

So, how do children learn to manage such a complex process for themselves? Prior to Hirsch's thesis, the philosopher George Herbert Mead had already attempted to describe how such understanding is constructed in early childhood, proposing that 'the self is something which has a development; it is not initially there at birth but arises in the process of social experience and activity... the self is essentially a social structure' (Mead 1934, p. 135). He developed a theory that he termed 'symbolic interactionism', in which make-believe play, during which children draw upon stories and events from the world in which they are immersed, plays a crucial part in the development of a socially connected 'self'.

Mead proposed that, for example, in making a cardboard box 'stand for' a pirate galleon or a towel for Batman's cape and, consequently, making the self a pirate or Batman, children become able to view the world from a flexible range of culturally relevant perspectives. While it is likely they have no real idea beyond a simple stereotype about how pirates or Batman behave, by playing 'let's pretend' with their culture's stories in this way, they take on different roles from the one that they inhabit as their 'real' self and, from this perspective, step outside the self and consider how it might feel to be someone else in the world in which they are becoming immersed.

> Narrative requires our unique capacity for meta-representation, not only to make and understand representations, but also to understand them *as* representations. This develops in children without training between their second and fifth years. Boyd (2009, p. 129)

Boyd's proposal is that young children have a natural urge to engage in such activities to develop the capacity for 'meta-representation' and, consequently, that the evolved human capacity to grasp ideas through the flexible manipulation of story underpinned by archetypal human narrative is an evolved behavior. In this sense, he is proposing that storying is essentially a 'primary skill' (Geary 2007); the adult provides the basic content rooted within a particular culture, and the child further 'works on it' through play, learning to move with increasing fluidity between underpinning narrative and specific story.

Jarvis (2006) observed children aged between four and six engaging in the natural primate style of chasing and catching but with the addition of culturally relevant narration to make human sense of the activities in which they were engaged. This play style has been found wherever play researchers have conducted investigations, for example, in non-Western cultures such as in the hunter–gatherer societies of the Khalahari Desert and in the ancient, multicultural environment of Oaxaca in Mexico (Jarvis 2019). Generations of British children will recognize the game as 'he', 'tig', or 'tag', depending on their regional origin (Opie and Opie 1969, p. 20), and it is also present within non-Anglophone post-industrial societies under a variety of names, such as 'El Dimoni' in Spain and 'Oni' in Japan (Jarvis 2019). Both of these words translate to 'devil' or 'demon', indicating the role that the catcher is perceived to take in the game, tapping into a pancultural archetype that can be traced back into pre-literate antiquity.

Jarvis (2006)'s child participants additionally added comprehensive make-believe to some of their chasing and catching play, drawn from stories that they had been introduced to both at home and at school, flexibly translating underpinning narratives, such as fear, heroic activity, and salvation into play relating to a wide range of contemporary media heroes and events of the time, such as Beyblades, Robot Wars, Batman, Disney Princesses, and even the primary hero of the English soccer team of that time, David Beckham. These children used gesture in parallel with verbalization to communicate meaning, including 'play face' (Konner 1972) and play intention signaling (Power 1999), exploring rudimentary non-verbal signaling. 'Narrative ... can operate through modes like mime, still pictures, shadow puppets or silent movies ... it need not be restricted to language' (Boyd 2018, p. 159).

In summary, there is evidence to suggest that, at a very young age, human beings become quite adept at 'storying' and that this is developed in a central element of their play with other children, drawing upon the underlying narratives in the stories to which they are introduced by adults and surrounding societal events. The urge to play at 'make-believe' with such cultural content appears to be naturally evolved. So, why might this have become an evolved feature via selection within the human species? What function might it fulfill?

3. What Is the Function of the Story?

The literary critic and educational theorist, Professor E. D. Hirsch emphasizes the importance of storytelling with young children, commenting that 'nothing is more universal and natural than the explicit communication of communal knowledge' (Hirsch 2016, p. 68). However, as previously indicated by McGuire (1990), Hirsch's take on what he dubs "cultural literacy" implies passivity in the learner, blurring the importance of active engagement with the contents of the story. Words only have meaning in context, however, and many words have more than one meaning. For example, do we eat a blackberry, or do we use it for texting people? Do we eat dates, or do we put them in our diaries? Moreover, what would a four-year-old's understanding of a 'raspberry pi' look like? Carroll (1871, online) archly explored this flexible element of language in an authoritative statement voiced by his pompous fictional character Humpty Dumpty: 'when I use a word, it means just what I choose it to mean, neither more nor less'. The child Alice replies, 'the question is whether you CAN make words mean so many different things', to which Humpty responds from the adult perspective: 'the question is which is to be master- that is all'.

A strong explanation for the function of stories in human development is the provision of a base for children to play with language during their developmental period in order to develop such mastery. Adults and societal events provide the raw materials for them to further shape this base in the collaborative make-believe activities outlined by Mead (1934) and Jarvis (2006). Adult-to-child transmission of story is only the first stage and must be followed by much further processing in order to develop full human competence and flexibility. The anthropology and history of childhood does not suggest passivity in the processing of cultural information through storying, particularly in the early years of life when children are learning how to manipulate story and narrative to make 'human sense' in the culture in which they are placed. Early childhood in hunter–gatherer and, later, rural societies of the past, including those of the Anglo-American West, involved listening to stories recounted by adults, observing societal events from an 'onlooker' child perspective, and many hours of free play with other children (Jarvis et al. 2017), in which make-believe was a universal play form (Mead 1934). More recent anthropological researchers propose that the roots of such behaviors are likely to be evolved in the natural selection of those whose cognitive architecture underpinned their ability to engage in such activities:

> A human cultural system may be immeasurably more complex than any game of pretend play. But just as a game is constructed out of pretend play tokens and rules, so human symbolic culture in general is composed entirely of entities constructed via a kind of play. Nettle (1999, pp. 232–33)

Harré (2002) gives a worked example of this phenomenon by comparing Snow White's magic mirror and Maui's magic fishhook to the 'magic' credit card he carries around in his pocket and the bank note that is really a valueless piece of paper containing a written promise, concluding that, in the human world, premised upon complex symbolic rules that underpin human understanding, 'material things have magic powers only in the contexts in which they are embedded' (Harré 2002, p. 25). This sets a daunting task for the human apprentice, learning to negotiate such a world in which all meaning is deeply immersed in symbology. Within this frame, children's participation in storying activities can be theorized as an evolved human vehicle for learning how to manipulate such an abstract system of meaning creation.

Emergent theory relating to the evolved nature of language and narrative is beginning to reveal the central importance of narrative and storytelling in human lives and human societies: 'storytelling appeals to our social intelligence. It arises out of our intense interest in monitoring one another and out of our evolved capacity to understand one another' (Boyd 2018, p. 383). Boyd proposes that stories foster cooperation by eliciting social and moral thought, as well as creativity, by requiring an individual to think beyond his or her immediate reality. Oatley (2016, p. 618) claims that engagement with fiction is the equivalent of 'taking in a piece of consciousness'.

Pellegrini and Galda (1990) propose that storytelling helps children to develop intersubjectivity and empathy with the emotions and motivations of others. Adams (1986, p. 4) comments that stories 'conspire with language' to produce a form of enjoyable instruction that is consistent with the culture in which the person is placed. This raises questions about the history of the story—how it works flexibly within culture to make meaning within time and place: 'the fairy tale offers a range of meanings ... [but] can only do that if it is itself structured around effect and if the child can identify with this structure' (McGuire 1990, p. 5). So, what examples can be provided to evidence this process?

4. The History of the Story

Bettelheim (1975, p. 45) proposed that folk and 'fairy' tales have a perennial purpose in addressing children's questions, such as 'what is the world really like? How am I to live my life in it?' He continues, 'like all great art, fairy tales both delight and instruct; their special genius is that they do so in terms which speak directly to children' (Bettelheim 1975, p. 53). As a Freudian, he suggests that some of the problems that characters within traditional folklore encounter may help children to contemplate some of their subconscious emotional concerns; for example, the cruelty of Cinderella's stepmother compared with the benevolence of the fairy godmother may allow children to contemplate their own mother from the perspective of both 'nice and nasty'. This evokes the psychoanalytic perspective of Melanie Klein, in which mothers (one of the most important Jungian archetypes) are integrated into the psyche as the source of both comfort and disappointment (Zaretsky 2005).

It has recently been suggested that some well-known European fairy tales were orally passed down through generations for at least 6000 years (Schultz 2016) prior to the introduction of printed versions. Native Australian grandparents continue in their traditional task of orally recounting the history of their culture to their grandchildren, in a traditional process known as 'Dadirri', which has been claimed to date back as far as 40,000 years (Ungunmerr-Baumann 1988). The concept of Dadirri is not fully translatable; however, it describes a process through which children are expected to develop quiet concentration and deep listening, paying close attention to the wisdom of their ancestors in order to become spiritually aware and socially responsible adults (Ungunmerr-Baumann 2002).

Several sources in Native Australian folklore accurately pinpoint flooding in areas that geographers now know experienced a dramatic raise in water levels between 12,000 and 9000 years ago, at the end of the last Ice Age: 'Garnguur, the seagull woman, took her raft and dragged it back and forth across the neck of the peninsula letting the sea pour in and making our homes into islands' (Reid and Nunn 2015, online). Floods of this nature happened all over the world at this time (Montgomery 2016), but Native Australian folk stories, recounted in the Dadirri process, are unique in their pinpointing of events to areas that correspond with modern geographical analysis.

Gough (1990) cites the very different example of the Xhosa people of South Africa, who have an oral storytelling tradition called iintsomi, in which the designated purpose is to create an original story from chunks of existing folklore, whilst still making narrative sense to the audience. This further illustrates the importance of cultural relevance in storytelling, which is also emphasized by McGuire (1990) and Adams (1986). 'Hearers expect their speakers to be relevant [and] their comprehension is based and calculated on this assumption' (Gough 1990, p. 200).

Many traditional Western folk stories, songs, and rhymes have more organically developed over time, matched to changing cultural conditions; in Western culture, this can most obviously be demonstrated by the ways in which stereotypical gender roles have changed in recent years and the manner in which Disney princesses changed alongside them, from the sweet, passive princesses of the 1950s films, such as *Snow White, Sleeping Beauty*, and *Cinderella*, to the feistier princesses of the early twenty-first century, such as the troubled, powerful ice queen Elsa in *Frozen*, her adventurous would-be-heroine sister Anna, and warrior Princess Merida in *Brave*.

There is also a clear, extended historical progression of traditional Western fairy stories in which details have gradually changed over centuries of retelling. For example, modern children would probably be highly disturbed by some of the first printed versions of *Hansel and Gretel, The Little Mermaid*, and *Cinderella* produced by the Brothers Grimm and Hans Christian Anderson in a century where harsh retribution was more public and commonplace. Hansel and Gretel kill the wicked witch by roasting her on her own fire, the Little Mermaid suffers pain and death as a consequence of her attempts to transcend her physical limitations, and Cinderella's stepsisters cut off their toes to fit the slipper with the prince only noticing the deception when their shoes fill with blood (Dawson and Tanaka 2018). This reflects Adams (1986) point about the necessity for stories to have an effective cultural meaning to their audience; hence, their existence within human culture not as a fixed phenomenon but as 'living, breathing entities, shifting in response to the needs of the community or listener' (Dawson and Tanaka 2018, p. xix). As McGuire (1990) points out, this problematizes Hirsch's concept of cultural stories 'fixing the vocabulary of a national culture' (Hirsch 1988, p. 84).

Wilson (2019, p. 43) reflects that 'when the environment changes, there is no reason to expect organisms to be well adapted to their new circumstances ... new adaptations [need] to evolve'. While stories are not living organisms, they are the cultural equivalent, the flexible carriers of the archetypal narrative, endlessly transformed by human beings to inform the next generation of universal 'truths' of what it is to be human but within a vehicle that is continually culturally crafted to fit the listener. So, how might stories be changing in our current culture, and what part does modern technology play?

5. The History of the Story: Embracing Technology?

Dawson (in Dawson and Tanaka 2018, p. xvii) makes the point that the current technological revolution is not the first such major change to impact the way in which human beings share stories, commenting that, over the eighteenth and nineteenth centuries, 'oral storytelling completed its almost total migration towards the written word, forever changing how we pass on knowledge and culture'. The flexibility of the story and its success in perpetuating the essential human narratives has endured, however.

The hero's journey (Campbell 2008) is a clear example of an archetypal narrative that can be followed through generations of diverse storying across a vast period of time in Western culture, during which orally transmitted tales were first committed to writing, then to print, and finally to film and interactive media: 'the hero is the man or woman who has been able to battle his past, his personal and local historical limitations ... to return transfigured and teach what he has learned of life' (Campbell 2008, pp. 14–15). Such a narrative is as clearly discerned in the ancient Greek tale of Odysseus as it is in modern 'journey of the hero' epics, such as Tolkien's published *Lord of the Rings* saga and Lucas' *Star Wars*, which was written and produced for the cinema. The journey of the Jedi knight Luke Skywalker has unfolded over a period of over forty years, both within the story itself and in real life (Galipeau 2001). Changing cultural conditions create the basis for continual reincarnations of the hero, morphing over many centuries from Odysseus sailing the Aegean in wooden ships to Luke Skywalker navigating the stars in his X-wing fighter. As such, it is a clear example of how such a fundamental human archetype is adapted for the audience over many centuries. While the narrative and its archetypal content may be perennial, the story belongs to the person who tells it and the culture and generation in which it is embedded.

The ancient 'distressed princess' is also an archetype that is commonly evoked in modern media and retold through a number of different stories, some drawing directly upon traditional Western stories, such as *Cinderella* and *Snow White*; some loosely based upon them, such as *Frozen* and its roots in Hans Christian Anderson's *The Snow Queen*; and some originally constructed for the cinema, for example *Brave*. Over a century of technological advancement, we have therefore begun to routinely communicate fundamental, panhuman, and very ancient narratives to young children through media, which can offer a far more visual and, more recently, technologically interactive world for the imagination than the traditional orally delivered presentation.

In terms of storying through dramatic performance, there is always the issue of appealing to both adult and child audiences. Willmott (2015, online) comments 'The art of pantomime humour used to be that it was risque [sic] enough to make the adults chuckle while the innuendo went over the kids' heads'. This introduces the concept of 'double coding'—a story that is narrated on different levels, carefully crafted for children of all ages and also for adults to enjoy by the extraction of different meanings. Obvious modern examples include double-coded jokes in cartoons in which children laugh at the obvious clowning and inadequacies of the characters, whilst adults engage with a far more deeply layered satire. For example, the world famous cartoon series *The Simpsons* introduced a cartoon-within-a-cartoon in *Itchy and Scratchy*—a violent TV program watched by the Simpson children that, to adult viewers, provides a biting satire of the *Tom and Jerry* cartoons that they watched as children and additionally:

> [M]ock[s] how contemporary society is dominated by the cultivation of a conspicuous consumer lifestyle through the importance of the idiot culture that "Ugly American" Homer Simpson relates to so well ... [whilst] using the cartoon-with-in-a-cartoon as a metaparodic device to play with the boundedness of the text as a text. Knox (2006, pp. 75–76)

There are long-standing debates about whether such conceptual 'layering' techniques were in fact always present within Western storytelling. For example, there is a long-standing debate over whether Cinderella's glass slipper—'verre' in French—was a mistranslation of 'vair' (fur) that arose as it began to be orally recounted in English. Dundes (1989) further commented that 'fur slipper' has been purported to be a sly reference to female genitalia. While traditional folk stories and rhymes originated within populations that were largely illiterate, the narrative that underpinned them was not necessarily simple or one-dimensional. For example, this deceptively childish rhyme has been proposed to contain both politically cynical and risqué messages for the adult audience of the time:

> I had a little nut tree
>
> Nothing would it bear
>
> But a silver nutmeg,
>
> And a golden pear;
>
> The King of Spain's daughter
>
> Came to visit me,
>
> And all for the sake
>
> Of my little nut tree

Gillespie (2012) proposes that 'the King of Spain's daughter' to which the rhyme refers was Catherine of Aragon, who came to England in 1501 to marry the oldest son of King Henry VII, Prince Arthur and that, as such:

> The golden pear turns into an expansive pun and joke that combines the notion of Arthur's lineage (the tree) and the golden pear (the royal womb). In other words, all that Arthur has to offer (and promise) is his semen, (the silver nutmeg), and an impregnated womb. The pear, or the womb, is gold because it will carry a royal child . . . In other words, the Little Nut Tree, the prince's genitalia, can produce nothing other than 'silver' semen and a 'golden' pear because of his royal lineage. Translation: The Little Nut Tree won't settle for anything less than an equally royal womb. The Prince must wait for a Princess. Gillespie (2012, online)

So, what of contemporary double coding? The first point to make is that, in the West, the contemporary cultural storying process has moved beyond the medium of print into sophisticated audiovisual mass media, presenting children not only with the highly visual messages that emerged from twentieth-century technological advances but also, since the early twenty-first century, associated interactive opportunities. There is evidence that, through this process, young children may be exposed to rather more intricately layered messages than they were in the storytelling of the past. For example, *The Lego Movie* weaves its story around the 'warrior discourse' (Jordan 1995, p. 75)—a perennial archetype often closely associated with the journey of the hero. In this modern guise, however, it contains a range of violent story lines bereft of human consequence. Lego characters 'die' in battle through a process in which they are cleanly disassembled into the pile of plastic bricks of which they are comprised, with an ongoing potential for reassembly. The story of the film elaborates on and jokes with respect to this process in the characters' fear of being glued together, thus curtailing their constant reincarnation via reconstruction. The final punchline revolves around a scene in which a powerful villain 'beheads' a character depicted as a spiritual leader, with the dialogue pitched towards adult cynicism when the disembodied head confesses that he was in fact a fraud all along.

This creates some potentially troubling messages for young children to absorb, in particular clean, stylized violence, which is removed from its consequences. This narrative is repeated in the *Lego Star Wars* games for iPad, in which the player becomes a Jedi knight wielding a light saber. While the intention of the programmers is clearly that the player should only behead the 'baddies', this requires the child to have quite a sophisticated grasp of the story underlying the game—pre-existing knowledge, which, in some cases, has been overestimated by the manufacturer. This issue stems from the remoteness of the adult storyteller, who not only narrates the tale bereft of contemporaneous interaction with the child audience but also dictates how the interactive element rooted in make-believe unfolds, which is often particularly constrained in games programmed for children under eight years of age. Additionally, the activities that are available in such games are typically undertaken by a solitary child in interaction with a machine rather than in collaboration with peers.

Might such modern sanitization of blood and death, based upon a technology in which Lego people neither bleed nor permanently die, blunt the messages originally carried by the earlier, conventionally communicated stories that Bettelhem suggested help children to prepare effectively for real life?

Additionally, the advent of such remote 'story products' could be extending the sanitization that initially occurred in the purged, printed fairy tales of the twentieth century, for example the versions of Cinderella in which the ugly sisters simply fail to fit their feet into the slipper and in which the little mermaid is able to transform her tail into legs via a benevolent magic spell. Willmott (2015, online) makes the point that, with respect to live pantomime performance, society has become obsessed with protecting children from negative or disturbing images, regardless of how accurately these reflect societal reality.

The princess narrative has recently been not only double- but multi-coded, ostensibly to disrupt traditional gender roles; however, traditional and 'new' narratives sometimes compete uneasily for supremacy within the structure of the story. For example, *Shrek*'s homely ogre Princess Fiona is by contrast extremely beautiful in her original non-cursed state, which she becomes able to inhabit at will, and while it is the sisterly love between Princesses Elsa and Anna in *Frozen* that has the strength to break a bad spell rather than the intervention of a savior prince, Elsa's magic nevertheless causes her to develop a far more mature (and sexually desirable) figure during her 'Let it Go' transformation (Stevens 2014). These are extremely sophisticated narratives to underpin stories created for very young children, containing potentially troubling cultural messages and perpetuating what Naomi Wolf calls 'the beauty myth' (Wolf 1991).

In the contemporary 'mediated' post-industrial world, then, young children are pitched into a deluge of densely layered, fast-moving audiovisual stories in which there may be no reality-relevant consequences emerging from the actions of the characters. Additionally, many such media products have given rise to associated adult-programmed interactive activities undertaken by solitary children, which share the 'no consequences' element and further extend it to the actions of the players themselves. In such modern 'mediated' fantasy worlds, women have a choice of when to be and when not to be beautiful with no obvious consequences, and there is no pain, blood, or death associated with physical violence.

Less 'sanitized' electronic games for older children may not create quite the same level of concern; for example, Cheryl Olson describes older children using more sophisticated gaming, frequently in multi-player formats, to work through feelings of fear, playing the game from different character perspectives to master the frightening content. She concludes that 'compared with other media such as books, films, and radio, electronic games appear to have an unusually expansive appeal and serve a surprising number of emotional, social, and intellectual needs' (Olson 2010, p. 185). It may therefore be that we have to take the player's age and developmental level quite carefully into account when carrying out research in this area and that it is specifically in the area of the lone-player fairytale-style games produced for younger children that the impact of online interaction needs to be most carefully explored. As Currie (2016, online) concludes, 'where I suspect this field of research is heading is to discover that some fictions are good for some people in some circumstances. Finding the which, who and what will take some time'. This will no doubt include online, interactive storying as technology continues to advance.

A key question can be focused on the ability (or not) of a young listener to provide ongoing feedback to the storyteller, which is hampered in our current society by the screen—the so-called 'fourth wall' between the storyteller and the audience. To reflect effectively upon this, we need to more deeply consider the organic nature of human language and storying—its dynamic exchange process that carries cultural messages between children and adults, allowing young children to meet, question, and collaboratively explore the complex ways in which human beings understand and operate in their world.

The concept of 'once upon a time' is so powerful for human beings that it is not just a traditional opening gambit in Western children's storybooks but an idea that can be detected in nearly every human language on Earth (Konnikova 2012). Is it as effectively articulated, however, through a modern audiovisual 'fourth wall' as it was in ancient legend, orally presented to children sitting around a campfire? This leaves us with many unanswered questions, such as the following:

- Do the commercialization and technologizing of ancient narrative into sanitized audiovisual stories and adult-programmed interactive games create a schism between young human beings and their evolved biological modes of storying?
- Is an organic element of human interaction lost in this process? Are commercialized adult-generated story products simply transmitted to and subsequently consumed by distant, solitary children, replacing the collaborative, organic 'in the moment' evolved human storying process?
- Is it possible that adults who do not receive ongoing feedback from child listeners via the evolved human communication process become isolated to the extent that they increasingly create over-sanitized and oversophisticated messages within modern, mediated storytelling for young children?

'Tens of thousands of years ago, when the human mind was young, and our numbers were few, we were telling one another stories' (Gottschall 2012, p. xiii). Our numbers are now much greater, and the ways in which we transmit our stories have greatly expanded. It may be that modern technology is fulfilling a vital role in this way, facilitating the much wider dissemination of human narrative. However, are the contemporary ways in which we reach so much further beyond ourselves than human beings of previous generations over-dictated by commercial imperatives and 'distant' technological media, removing much of the organic experience from the process? Moreover, what implications might this have for such a highly socially dependent species, which despite its technological wizardry, remains 'Homo Sapiens 1.0' (Bishop 2012), heavily reliant upon the ability to collaboratively construct, understand, and communicate cohesive narratives to create and sustain cooperative societies?

6. Modern Life and the Story

The fact that storytelling still holds a crucial place in human lives is reflected in our giant multinational entertainment franchises; however, in the past, storying held a greater potential for young children to ground and explore their own imaginations, both in direct interaction with the storyteller and subsequently by using ideas drawn from stories to play with the underlying narratives in social free play with other children. While modern children may be the first generation to personally interact with the characters and events in their favorite stories through the magic of technology, such engagement is inevitably scripted by adults via the programming of the product, which limits young children's potential for creativity and moves such interaction into a solitary event, which takes place outside of the natural environment.

Additionally, opportunities for Western children's active independent free play have gradually declined over recent decades, which has resulted in less freedom for children aged between five and twelve years to 'roam' unsupervised by adults around public areas in the close vicinity of their homes. A subsequent plethora of adult-structured and -supervised activities, both conventional and technically mediated have arisen, purportedly to keep children 'safe' whilst parents work for long hours within neoliberal economies. A growing focus on academic achievement has additionally resulted in less time allocated for children to engage in active collaborative free play during their school day (Jarvis 2019). Upstart Scotland (2018, online) posed the following question to parents of young children: 'When was the last time you heard the shouts, squeals and laughter of children as they ran, jumped, climbed, built dens, made mixtures and played "let's pretend" in their local neighbourhood?' Such silence provides a sharp contrast with the findings of mid-twentieth-century play researchers Peter and Iona Opie:

> There is no town or city known to us where street games do not flourish ... To understand the "wanton sports" of the Elizabethan day, and the horseplay of even earlier times is to watch the contemporary child engrossed in his traditional pursuits on the metalled floor of a twentieth-century city. (Opie and Opie 1969, p. ix)

Jarvis et al. (2014) suggested that social free play deprivation during the developmental period may result in social disconnectedness amongst a species that has evolved to live within highly socially connected environments. Bruner (1976, p. 56) commented, 'development which is separated from a natural social environment 'provides no guide, only knowledge ... These are the conditions for alienation and confusion'.

Jarvis (2019, p. 323) considers potential 'fall-out' from such a sudden generational change:

> In September 2012, the British newspaper the Daily Telegraph reported that 'A "cotton wool culture" of over-protecting children has contributed to a decline in freedom for them to play' ... a "shocking" half of children aged between seven and 12 were not allowed to climb a tree without an adult present and one in five children of the same age had been stopped from playing conkers because it was "too dangerous".

In 2017, the same newspaper reported again on the same generation, now teenagers, outlining a growing public concern that young people were 'perceived to be over-sensitive and intolerant of disagreement' (Jarvis 2019, p. 323).

Psychologist Gray (2011) has no doubt about the negative effects of decreasing opportunities for children to engage in collaborative, independent free play in natural environments, proclaiming that our current modes of raising children are unnatural and, consequently, produce adults who lack social and emotional skills, which he further poses as an explanation for the recent increase in mental breakdowns amongst young people. Wilson (2019, p. 73) also reflects on the problems that may arise as natural play modes disappear from children's lives: 'with disruptions of child development we are faced with the tragic possibility that we are harming our own children, based on our lack of biological knowledge'.

'Storying' has, however, not featured very highly in such explanations, and there has been little research specifically focused upon the ways in which it acts as both adhesive and lubricant in the social interactions of children engaged in collaborative free play. Some practice-based research has documented the importance of storying in the classroom; for example, Paley (1984, 1991, 2005) describes the ways in which children use stories to negotiate their lives in the early stages of primary school, while Nicolopoulou et al. (2015) found that participation in a storytelling and story-acting practice was associated with improvements in narrative comprehension, print and word awareness, pretend abilities, self-regulation, and reduced play disruption, but these studies were facilitated through a relatively fixed, adult-imposed, and classroom-based agenda.

The development of modern technology has undoubtedly brought many advantages to humanity, but we have not yet thought deeply enough about the ways in which hurried 'mediated' modern lifestyles may impact young human beings who come into the world equipped with the same psychobiological needs as their Ice Age ancestors. If we wish to nurture human development of sociability, flexibility, and creativity, we might be well advised to make deliberate time and space in children's lives for collaborative free play and for face-to-face storytelling, both in the home and in the primary school. The application of Tinbergen's questions relating to the development, function, and history of storying (Wilson 2019) suggests that we have not yet effectively considered the evolved role of storying in the development of a fully symbolically, socially, and creatively competent human being. Stories are a natural food for the human mind, and perhaps, cultivating both the listening and creativity skills that are evoked by organic engagement with human storying is as conducive to the health of the human mind as natural foods are to the health of the body.

Gottschall (2012, p. xiv) reflects, 'story for humans is as water to a fish-all-encompassing and not quite palpable'. Does this in turn make it difficult for us to unravel 'the story of the story' in the evolution of humanity and to effectively reflect upon the impact that relatively rapid, radical changes in modes of transmission may have upon our species? While it is clearly counterproductive to take a wholly negative orientation to modern technological innovation, it is likely that we would benefit from becoming more consciously aware of the evolved ways in which human beings have, for many centuries, introduced their children to the organic human phenomenon of narrative and 'storying' and how this might be more effectively harnessed to consciously and explicitly nurture healthy social development and emergent flexible creativity.

Funding: This research received no external funding.

Conflicts of Interest: The author declares no conflict of interest.

References

Adams, Jeff. 1986. *The Conspiracy of the Text: The Place of Narrative in the Development of Thought*. London: Routledge and Kegan Paul.

Bateson, Mary. 1975. Mother–infant exchanges: The epigenesis of conversational interaction. In *Developmental Psycholinguistics and Communication Disorders: Annals of the New York Academy of Sciences*. Edited by Doris Aaronson and Robert W. Rieber. New York: New York Academy of Sciences, vol. 263.

Bettelheim, Bruno. 1975. *The Uses of Enchantment: The Meaning and Importance of Fairy Tales*. London: Peregrine.

Bishop, Todd. 2012. Remembering Bill Hill: The most important operating system is Homo Sapiens 1.0. *Geek Wire*, October 18. Available online: https://www.geekwire.com/2012/remembering-bill-hill-important-operating-system-homo-sapiens-10/ (accessed on 1 August 2019).

Boyd, Brian. 2009. *On the Origin of Stories*. Harvard: Harvard University Press.

Boyd, Brian. 2018. The evolution of stories: From mimesis to language, from fact to fiction. *Wiley Interdisciplinary Reviews: Cognitive Science* 9: e1444. Available online: https://onlinelibrary.wiley.com/doi/epdf/10.1002/wcs.1444 (accessed on 1 August 2019). [CrossRef] [PubMed]

Bronfenbrenner, Uri, and Stephen Ceci. 1994. Nature-Nurture Reconceptualised in Developmental Perspective: A Bio-Ecological Model. *Psychological Review* 107: 568–86. [CrossRef]

Bruner, Jerome. 1976. Nature and uses of Immaturity. In *Play: Its Role in Development and Evolution*. Edited by Jerome S. Bruner, Alison Jolly and Kathy Sylva. New York: Basic Books, pp. 28–64.

Bruner, Jerome. 1990. *Acts of Meaning*. Cambridge: Harvard.

Bruner, Jerome. 1991. The Narrative Construction of Reality. *Critical Enquiry* 18: 1–21. [CrossRef]

Bruner, Jerome. 1996. *The Culture of Education*. Cambridge: Harvard.

Campbell, Joseph. 2008. *The Hero with a Thousand Faces*, 3rd ed. Novato: New World Library.

Carroll, Lewis. 1871. Alice Through the Looking Glass. Available online: https://www.gutenberg.org/ebooks/12 (accessed on 1 August 2019).

Chase, Philip. 1999. Symbolism as a reference and symbolism as a culture. In *The Evolution of Culture*. Edited by Robin Dunbar, Chris Knight and Camilla Power. Edinburgh: Edinburgh University Press, pp. 34–49.

Currie, Gregory. 2016. Can reading fiction literally change your mind? *The Conversation (online)*, July 20. Available online: https://theconversation.com/can-reading-fiction-literally-change-your-mind-62726 (accessed on 1 August 2019).

Dawson, Willow, and Shelley Tanaka. 2018. *White as Milk, Red as Blood*. Toronto: Alfred A. Kopf.

Dunbar, Robin, Chris Knight, and Camilla Power. 1999. *The Evolution of Culture*. Edinburgh: Edinburgh University Press.

Dundes, Alan. 1989. *Folklore Matters*. Knoxville: University of Tennessee Press.

Galipeau, Steven. 2001. *The Journey of Luke Skywalker: An Analysis of Modern Myth and Symbol*. Peru: Open Court.

Geary, David. 1998. *Male, Female, The Evolution of Human Sex Differences*. Washington, DC: American Psychological Association.

Geary, David. 2007. *Educating the Evolved Mind: Conceptual Foundations for an Evolutionary Educational Psychology*. Charlotte: Information Age Publishing.

Gillespie, Patrick. 2012. I had a little nut tree . . . . *PoemShape*, June 4. Available online: https://poemshape.wordpress.com/2012/06/04/i-had-a-little-nut-tree/ (accessed on 1 August 2019).

Gottschall, Jonathan. 2012. *The Story Telling Animal*. Boston: Mariner.

Gough, David. 1990. The principle of relevance and the production of discourse: Evidence from Xhosa folk narrative. In *Narrative Thought and Narrative Language*. Edited by Bruce Britton and Anthony Pellegrini. Mahwah: Laurence Erlbaum, pp. 199–218.

Gray, Peter. 2011. The Decline of Play and the Rise of Psychopathology in Children and Adolescents. *American Journal of Play* 3: 443–63.

Harré, Rom. 2002. Material Objects in Social Worlds. *Theory, Culture and Society* 19: 23–33. [CrossRef]

Hirsch, Eric Donald. 1967. *Validity in Interpretation*. New Haven: Yale University Press.

Hirsch, Eric Donald. 1988. *Cultural Literacy*. New York: Vintage.

Hirsch, Eric Donald. 2016. *Why Knowledge Matters*. Cambridge: Harvard.
Jarvis, Pam. 2006. Rough and Tumble Play, Lessons in Life. *Evolutionary Psychology* 4: 268–86. [CrossRef]
Jarvis, Pam. 2019. A place to play: Online and offline in the twenty first century. In *Perspectives on Play: Learning for Life*. Edited by Avril Brock, Pam Jarvis and Yinka Olusoga. Abingdon: Routledge, pp. 314–38.
Jarvis, Pam, Stephen Newman, and Louise Swiniarski. 2014. On 'becoming social': The importance of collaborative free play in childhood. *International Journal of Play* 3: 53–68. Available online: http://research.leedstrinity.ac.uk/files/161043/Jarvis_Newman_Swiniarski_On_becoming_social_August_2013.pdf (accessed on 1 August 2019). [CrossRef]
Jarvis, Pam, Louise Swiniarski, and Wendy Holland. 2017. *Early Years Pioneers in Context: Their Lives, Lasting Influence and Impact on Practice Today*. Abingdon: Routledge.
Jordan, Ellen. 1995. Fighting Boys and Fantasy Play: The Construction of Masculinity in the Early Years of School. *Gender and Education* 7: 69–87. [CrossRef]
Jung, Carl Gustav. 2003. *Four Archetypes*. Abingdon: Routledge.
Knox, Simone. 2006. Reading the Ungraspable Double-Codedness of The Simpsons. *Journal of Popular Film and Television* 34: 73–81. Available online: https://www.tandfonline.com/doi/abs/10.3200/JPFT.34.2.73-81 (accessed on 1 August 2019). [CrossRef]
Konner, Melvin. 1972. Aspects of the Developmental Ethology of a Foraging People. In *Ethological Studies of Child Behaviour*. Edited by Nicholas Blurton Jones. Cambridge: Cambridge University Press, pp. 285–304.
Konnikova, Maria. 2012. The Power of Once upon a Time: A Story to Tame the Wild Things. *Scientific American*, May 8. Available online: https://blogs.scientificamerican.com/literally-psyched/the-power-of-once-upon-a-time-a-story-to-tame-the-wild-things/ (accessed on 1 August 2019).
Low, Bobbi. 1989. Cross Cultural Patterns in the Training of Children: An Evolutionary Perspective. *Journal of Comparative Psychology* 103: 311–19. [CrossRef] [PubMed]
Lyle, Sue. 2000. Narrative Understanding: Developing a Theoretical Context for Understanding how Children Make Meaning in Classroom Settings. *Journal of Curriculum Studies* 32: 45–63. [CrossRef]
Mallon, Ron, and Stephen Stich. 2000. The Odd Couple: The Compatibility of Social Constructionism and Evolutionary Psychology. *Philosophy of Science* 67: 133–54. [CrossRef]
McGuire, Michael. 1990. The Rhetoric of Narrative: A hermeneutic critical theory. In *Narrative Thought and Narrative Language*. Edited by Bruce Britton and Anthony Pellegrini. Mahwah: Lawrence Erlbaum, pp. 219–36.
Mead, George Herbert. 1934. *Mind, Self and Society*. Chicago: University of Chicago Press.
Montgomery, David. 2016. Geomythology: Can geologists relate ancient stories of great floods to real events? *The Conversation*, August 15. Available online: https://theconversation.com/geomythology-can-geologists-relate-ancient-stories-of-great-floods-to-real-events-63434 (accessed on 1 August 2019).
Nettle, Daniel. 1999. Language variation and the evolution of societies. In *The Evolution of Culture*. Edited by Robin Dunbar, Chris Knight and Camilla Power. Edinburgh: Edinburgh University Press, pp. 214–27.
Nicolopoulou, Ageliki, Kai Schnabel Cortina, Hande Ilgaz, Carolyn Brockmeyer Cates, and Aline B. de Sá. 2015. Using a narrative- and play-based activity to promote low-income preschoolers' oral language, emergent literacy, and social competence. *Early Child Research Questions* 31: 147–62. Available online: https://www.ncbi.nlm.nih.gov/pmc/articles/PMC4391821/pdf/nihms-665638.pdf (accessed on 1 August 2019). [CrossRef] [PubMed]
Oatley, Keith. 2016. Fiction: Simulation of Social Worlds. *Trends in Cognitive Sciences* 20: 618–28. Available online: https://www.cell.com/trends/cognitive-sciences/fulltext/S1364-6613(16)30070-5?_returnURL=https%3A%2F%2Flinkinghub.elsevier.com%2Fretrieve%2Fpii%2FS1364661316300705%3Fshowall%3Dtrue (accessed on 1 August 2019). [CrossRef]
Olson, Cheryl. 2010. Children's motivations for video game play in the context of normal development. *Review of General Psychology* 13: 180–87. [CrossRef]
Opie, Iona, and Peter Opie. 1969. *Children's Games in Street and Playground*. London: Oxford University Press.
Paley, Vivian. 1984. *Boys and Girls, Superheroes in the Doll Corner*. Chicago: University of Chicago Press.
Paley, Vivian. 1991. *The Boy Who Would be a Helicopter: Uses of Storytelling in the Classroom*. Harvard: Harvard University Press.
Paley, Vivian. 2005. *A Child's Work: The Importance of Fantasy Play*. Chicago: University of Chicago Press.

Pellegrini, Anthony, and Lee Galda. 1990. The Joint Construction of Stories by Pre-School Children and an Experimenter. In *Narrative Thought and Narrative Language*. Edited by Bruce Britton and Anthony Pellegrini. Mahwah: Lawrence Erlbaum, pp. 113–30.

Power, Thomas. 1999. *Play and Exploration in Children and Animals*. Mahwah: Lawrence Erlbaum.

Reid, Nick, and Patrick Nunn. 2015. Ancient Aboriginal stories preserve history of a rise in sea level. *The Conversation*, January 12. Available online: https://theconversation.com/ancient-aboriginal-stories-preserve-history-of-a-rise-in-sea-level-36010 (accessed on 1 August 2019).

Schultz, David. 2016. Some fairy tales may be 6000 years old. *Science Online*, April 22. Available online: https://www.sciencemag.org/news/2016/04/some-fairy-tales-may-be-6000-years-old?utm_source=social_media&utm_medium=hootsuite&utm_campaign=standard&utm_source=hootsuite&utm_medium=social&utm_campaign=standard (accessed on 1 August 2019).

Stevens, Dana. 2014. I can't let it go. *The Slate*. Available online: https://slate.com/culture/2014/02/let-it-go-idina-menzels-frozen-ballad-it-sends-the-wrong-message.html (accessed on 1 August 2019).

Swearingen, C. Jan. 1990. The Narration of Dialogue and Narration of within Dialogue: The transition from story to Logic. In *Narrative Thought and Narrative Language*. Edited by Bruce Britton and Anthony Pellegrini. Mahwah: Lawrence Erlbaum, pp. 173–98.

Tinbergen, Niko. 1963. On Aims and Methods of Ethology. *Zeitschrift Fur Tierpsychologie* 20: 410–33. [CrossRef]

Tomasello, Michael. 1999. *The Cultural Origins of Human Cognition*. Cambridge: Harvard.

Ungunmerr-Baumann, Miriam Rose. 1988. Dadirri: Inner Deep Listening and Quiet Still Awareness. Available online: https://www.miriamrosefoundation.org.au/about-dadirri/dadirri-text (accessed on 1 August 2019).

Ungunmerr-Baumann, Miriam Rose. 2002. Dadirri—A Reflection. Available online: http://nextwave.org.au/wp-content/uploads/Dadirri-Inner-Deep-Listening-M-R-Ungunmerr-Bauman-Refl.pdf (accessed on 1 August 2019).

Upstart Scotland. 2018. The Silence of the Weans. Available online: https://www.upstart.scot/the-silence-of-the-weans/ (accessed on 1 August 2019).

Willmott, Phil. 2015. How to Write a Pantomime. *The Stage (online)*, December 3. Available online: https://www.thestage.co.uk/advice/how-to/2015/phil-willmott-how-to-write-a-pantomime/ (accessed on 1 August 2019).

Wilson, David Sloan. 2019. *This View of Life: Completing the Darwinian Revolution*. Toronto: Pantheon.

Wolf, Naomi. 1991. *The Beauty Myth*. London: Vintage.

Yoo, Huynjoo, Dale Bowman, and Oller D. Kimbrough. 2018. The Origin of Protoconversation: An Examination of Caregiver Responses to Cry and Speech-Like Vocalizations. *Frontiers in Psychology* 9: 1510. Available online: https://www.frontiersin.org/articles/10.3389/fpsyg.2018.01510/full (accessed on 1 August 2019). [CrossRef] [PubMed]

Zaretsky, Eli. 2005. *Secrets of the Soul: A Social and Cultural History of Psychoanalysis*. New York: Vintage.

Zeedyk, Suzanne. 2006. From intersubjectivity to subjectivity: The transformative roles of emotional intimacy and imitation. *Infant and Child Development* 15: 321–44. [CrossRef]

© 2019 by the author. Licensee MDPI, Basel, Switzerland. This article is an open access article distributed under the terms and conditions of the Creative Commons Attribution (CC BY) license (http://creativecommons.org/licenses/by/4.0/).

Article

Schooled for Servitude: The Education of African Children in British Colonies, 1910–1990

Mark Malisa [1,*] and Thelma Quardey Missedja [2]

[1] Educational Research and Administration, University of West Florida, Pensacola, FL 32514, USA
[2] Educational Studies (Instructional Technology), Ohio University, Athens, GA 45701, USA
* Correspondence: mmalisa@uwf.edu

Received: 7 May 2019; Accepted: 5 July 2019; Published: 11 July 2019

Abstract: Our paper examines the education of African children in countries that were colonized by Britain, including Ghana, South Africa, and Zimbabwe. We show how education plays an important role in shaping and transforming cultures and societies. Although the colonies received education, schools were segregated according to race and ethnicity, and were designed to produce racially stratified societies, while loyalty and allegiance to Britain were encouraged so that all felt they belonged to the British Empire or the Commonwealth. In writing about the education of African children in British colonies, the intention is not to convey the impression that education in Africa began with the arrival of the colonizers. Africans had their own system and history of education, but this changed with the incursion by missionaries, educators as well as conquest and colonialism.

Keywords: colonialism; apartheid; Africa; social reproduction; racism

1. Introduction

Our paper examines the education of African children in countries that were colonized by Britain, with a focus on South Africa, while general observations are made about other African countries colonized by Britain. Through providing a historical overview of education in former British colonies, we also present a 'genealogy of education in the colonies.' Although the focus of our paper is on education in former British colonies, we also highlight the role of the United States' educational policies and their influence in colonial Africa. The impact of the United States' educational policies is detectable in African colonial education, and in different historical periods, experts from the United States were consulted on matters related to the education of Africans. In the early part of the 19th and 20th Centuries, the education of African Americans had a bearing on the education of Africans in British colonies (Loram 1927; Yamada 2008). In both contexts, race and racism played a huge role in the education of Black children (Curry 2009; Jansen 1996; Margo 1986). In this paper, we also show how Plessy vs. Ferguson provided a blueprint for apartheid education in South Africa, just as the Brown vs. Board of Education influenced educational policies in postcolonial countries.

Genealogy, in this context, refers to studying the history and origins of a system. For example, there are studies on the genealogy of law (Clark and Lauderdale 2012) and political authority (French 2011) among other things. However, genealogy itself is also a way of conducting research (Vucetic 2011). As such, in this paper, we examine a history or genealogy of education in former British colonies in Africa.

Education plays an important role in shaping and transforming cultures and societies (Appel 2004; Armah 2008; Bowles and Gintis 1976; Mandela 1994; Pinar and Bowers 1992). Although the colonies received education, schools were segregated according to race and ethnicity, while loyalty and allegiance to Britain were encouraged so that all felt they belonged to the British Empire or the Commonwealth (Boampong 2013; Mandela 1994). In writing about the education of African children in British colonies, the intention is not to convey the impression that education in Africa began with the arrival of the colonizers. Africans had their own system and history of education, but this changed with the incursion by missionaries as well as conquest and colonialism (Bude 1983; Diop 1974; Wa Thiongo 2008).

Colonial governments made education available to African children, ranging from eight years and above. However, there were very few schools for African children, and as such, only a small section of the population attended formal schooling (Armah 1972; Wa Thiongo 2014). Colonial education, in many ways, was an important component of colonizing the mind, and the curriculum played an important role. We point out, at the onset, that even though Europeans did not "introduce education to [West] Africa what they did bring were their own particular methods of instruction and their subject matter content. Western education molded minds along different lines than did indigenous African education" (Corby 1990, p. 314). In other words, a new type of education took place with the colonization of Africa.

We also highlight how the colonial curriculum was designed to educate African children to take up subordinate roles. Although the curriculum was designed to foster subservience to Europeans and loyalty to Britain, schools in Africa ended up being centers for revolutionary protest, and birthplaces of liberation movements (Armah 2008; Malisa 2010). The colonial curriculum created an image of civilized Africans as those who had assimilated into European culture. Such Africans ended up with a different sort of values, often conflicting with indigenous cultures and understandings of childhood (Armah 2008; Salazar 2013; Mandela 1994).

For the most part, the targets of colonial education were children, ranging from those in elementary to secondary school (Bude 1983; Ofori-Attah 2006; Omolewa 2006). The curriculum, often imported from either Britain or North America, was intentionally designed to produce Africans who would have an inferiority complex when it came to their interaction with Europeans. In addition, such educated Africans were to be content working for Europeans, and when placed in positions of authority, would ensure that other Africans continued to serve the interests of the colonizer (Mandela 1994). A significant part of our work is on South Africa, a British colony, which only gained independence in 1992.

2. Method

This article uses document analysis as a qualitative research method to examine the education of African children in British colonies. The analysis of the data in qualitative research enables researchers to delve into and understand the behaviors, experiences, and meanings that people attach to the phenomenon under study (Sutton and Austin 2015). Many researchers (Creswell and Poth 2018; Glesne 2016; Patton 2015; Thomas et al. 2015) have identified the sources of data in qualitative research as interviews, observations, documents, and audiovisuals.

Documents are a source of data that a researcher can use to support a study. Documents may be electronic or printed (Bowen 2009). The information in documents is not normally produced by the researcher but may be a compilation of images and texts that record issues, experiences, regulations etc. (Bowen 2009; Schensul et al. 1999). Documents may be (a) primary, consisting of fieldnotes from participant observations, interview transcripts, photographs to mention a few, or (b) secondary, consisting of demographic data, records, surveys, database information and many more (Schensul et al. 1999). Per O'Leary (2014), documents are primarily in three forms: public records, personal documents, and physical evidence. Public records consist of reports, handbooks, institutional/company websites, syllabi, etc.; personal documents consist of emails, blogs, individual websites, journals etc.; physical evidence consist of photographs, artifacts, posters, etc. (Bogdan and Biklen 2006; Bowen 2009; O'Leary 2014). In this article, we utilize public records, personal documents, syllabi, and literature.

Document analysis is a process of examining and interpreting documents (electronic or printed) systematically to gain understanding and knowledge (Bowen 2009; Altheide and Schneider 2013). Analyzing documents involves coding information to develop themes in order to draw realistic conclusions or meanings (Altheide and Schneider 2013; Bengtsson 2016; Bowen 2009). Per Bowen (2009), document analysis is often used to corroborate findings from other data sources such as interviews in a process called triangulation. Our sources of data, as such, are different documents. In keeping with document analysis, we examine the themes that emerge from the literature, from the documents.

Documents used in the article included official government papers, especially documents regarding apartheid education. The literature on the Eiselen Commission and the Bantu Education Act is publicly available and accessible, and it captures the educational policies of South Africa in the period after 1948. Likewise, the Plessy vs. Ferguson documents are publicly accessible. In addition to government policies and court documents, there is ample literature on education during the colonial era. Such literature includes autobiographical texts, including the autobiography of Mandela (1994). Tracts or pamphlets from missionaries as well as novels and historical fiction also chronicle education in British colonies. Many of the novels and historical fiction by Ayi Kwei Armah of Ghana and Ngugi Wa Thiongo from Kenya are primarily critiques of colonial education. Loram's book, written in 1927, provides a comprehensive analysis and comparison between education in South Africa and the United States. The books and documents listed above are cited and appear in the reference section of this paper.

3. Colonialism and the Education of African Children

The 1884 Berlin Conference created different countries in Africa, and blanketed the continent under different European countries, including Britain, France, Germany, and Belgium, among others (Armah 2010). Colonialism and colonial education remained intact up to the time different African nations gained political independence. Colonial education in Africa was undertaken by separate entities, each with its own purposes. These included missionaries, merchants, and foreign or colonial governments.

When the missionaries sought to educate Africans, their main purpose was to have Africans who could help during worship times. According to Omolewa, the missionaries saw education as useful for training Africans to help the missionaries. As such, those Africans who were educated could become catechists or messengers (Omolewa 2006). Rarely were Africans allowed to become priests, especially prior to the 20th century. Mission schools could be found in different parts of each colonized country, depending on which Christian denomination had settled in that part. Among missionaries, education was acknowledged as an important tool for mission evangelization: "Mission societies therefore endeavored to redevelop aspects of mission education and adapt to the changing sociopolitical environment, while protecting space for religious education" (Yamada 2008, p. 23).

In addition to missionaries, traders or merchants also provided education to Africans. This kind of education was designed to produce Africans who would help the merchants with administering foreign business or the business interests of the colonizers. Such an education happened at a very low scale, and only a very small percentage of the African population received an education. Merchants sometimes worked with the missionaries in shaping the curriculum (Ofori-Attah 2006; Omolewa 2006).

Just as missionaries and merchants had a vested interest in the education of Africans, colonial governments also saw an advantage in educating a small section of the African population, including the sons of chiefs. To help in the administration of the colonies, the British "founded a number of schools throughout their African colonial empire to educate sons of chiefs for positions of inferiority" (Corby 1990, p. 319). It was not uncommon for the colonial administration to pick the most callous of the chiefs' sons and train them to take up jobs as servants of the empire (Armah 2000, p. 1972). Such sons were identified while they were relatively young, before they reached their teens.

Over time, neither the Africans nor the colonial agents (missionaries, merchants, and colonial governments) were happy with the quality of education as well as the result of colonial education. One major problem was the inherent nature of racism in the educational system. In most colonies, schools were segregated: there were some for Africans, and some for Europeans. Schools for European (White) students were better when compared with those for Africans (Blacks). In general, colonial governments created educational systems for propagating the advantages of European students while educating Africans for subservient positions (Walker and Archung 2003). The aim of colonial education was that:

> The brown workman would always have to work under a European and therefore there would be no conflict. The cast of mind of the Native is such that he could rarely take charge. His lack of inventiveness and of ingenuity in mechanical work would make him inferior to the European as a trained workman, and at no time would he compete with the European. (Roberts 1905, p. 804)

However, with more education, Africans became restive and resisted colonialism. Schools became places for political unrest as Africans sought to end colonialism. The British also seemed to regret and doubt whether they had achieved their aims. Those who participated in the Phelps-Stokes Fund (an organization made of British and North American educators who focused on Africa) observed that mission boys represented "the futility and harm of educating natives away from 'their place' in the colonial scheme arranged by western civilization for the Africans. (Jones 1925, p. 249 as cited in Yamada 2008, p. 23).

4. British and North American Influences on Educational Policies in Colonial Africa

Aspects of colonial education were adapted or imported from Britain and North America (Yamada 2008). This importation should not come as a major surprise, especially as the missionaries, merchants, and colonial administrators came from those countries. Missionaries from Britain and North America, for example, took it upon themselves to go and educate Africans (Armah 1972; Bude 1983). To a great extent, North American policies had a bigger influence in the education policies in colonial Africa. In the Southern United States, Jim Crow Laws were regarded as the norm, and the Plessey vs. Ferguson decision of 1896 (also referred to as Separate but Equal) left Blacks vulnerable to the whims of White Americans, and schools as well as other public institutions, remained segregated. Plessey vs. Ferguson, to a great extent, provided the blueprint for apartheid education in South Africa, and the normalization of racial segregation in schools.

Scholars observe that in the 19th and 20th centuries, American models of industrial education were imported to many African colonies (Persianis 1996; Yamada 2008). After the emancipation of slaves, the United States sought to educate African Americans, but with the type of education that would make African Americans subservient to Whites. As Fosdick put it, "if the white southerners had to permit the Negro to obtain any education at all, they wanted it to be of the sort that would make him a better servant and laborer, not that which would train him to rise out of his place" (as cited in Yamada 2008, p. 26). That racial component was transferred to the education in the colonies, especially in South Africa. South Africa was colonized, first by the Dutch, then the British (Chisholm 1983; Paterson 2005). Each introduced a different educational system.

According to Loram (1927), there were similarities between the racism in South Africa and the United States since educators claimed that the "backwardness of the Southern States in the United States is partly attributable to the presence of masses of uneducated Negroes, who are dragging down the whites to a lower level, socially, politically, and economically. Signs of similar degeneration on the parts of the whites in South Africa are not wanting," (p. 12). Several legal measures were put in place to make it difficult or almost impossible for African children to get a quality education in British colonies.

One of the ways for disenfranchising Africans or denying them access to education was through prohibiting them from voting. Without the right to vote, Africans had no mechanisms for redressing the challenges that African children faced regarding quality education. Because the economic situation demanded that Africans be dependent on a cash economy, most found themselves with their labor as the only commodity they could trade (Chisholm 1983; Johnson 1982). At times the labor pool was such that Africans worked almost for free, while their children could not afford an education. In other words, African parents could rarely afford to spend time with their own children because they were providing cheap labor to Europeans living in the colonies. Loram (1927) observes:

> Visitors to South Africa are struck by our complete dependence upon cheap Native labor. No one is too poor to afford a Zulu 'boy' to do housework which is done by mothers and

daughters in the European countries; the 'boy' carries the schoolgirl's satchel of books to school and the workman's bag of tools, (p. 11).

While South African blacks provided cheap labor, there were additional legislations that made it difficult for Africans and African children to have access to the same resources as Europeans in British colonies. The Natives in Urban Areas Bill of 1918 restricted areas where Blacks could live. The legislation was later replaced by the Group Areas Act. The legislations governing race relations in South Africa and most of the British colonies closely resembled those in Separate but Equal legislation based on the Plessy vs. Ferguson decision in the United States (Roche 1951). Roche (1951) viewed Separate but Equal as "the prototype for the current apartheid program of the Union of South" (p. 219).

Just as was the case in the United States, in British colonies, racial segregation was, for the most part, presumed to be the norm. Beittel (1951) viewed segregation in schools and in life as a form of ostracism designed to keep Blacks at the bottom of the social and economic ladder. It created and supported a racial caste system that divided the nation, and indeed, the world. However, there were other long-term and unintended consequences. Margo (1986) contends that the achievement gap, to a great extent, can be traced to Separate but Equal. According to Margo (1986), "low black incomes, wealth, and high rates of adult illiteracy helped sustain a significant racial achievement gap even if separate-but-equal were reality instead of myth" (p. 794).

The struggles for racial integration and school desegregation in the British colonies in Africa closely mirrored those in Britain, even those dealing with the Irish (Hickman 1993). The Anglicization of White children who were not British was carried out in South Africa as well. After the British settlers defeated the Dutch or Afrikaans, Dutch ceased to be the language of instruction, and the curriculum in schools was drastically changed (Johnson 1982). Thus, in many ways, schools normalized whiteness as the standard by which children could have access to quality education, and whiteness was generally reserved for White and British Europeans. A person was British, not by virtue of citizenship and birth, but largely by the color of their skin. It should also be noted that leading British intellectuals of the day championed colonialism as a way to contain the race problem in Britain (Curry 2009). For Curry, Royce's disposition toward Blacks was firmly rooted in a "colonial and assimilationist logic that that ultimately sought the cultural destruction of African-descended people" (2009, p. 11). There was thus a concerted effort to deculturize Africans while conditioning them to provide labor to Europeans. Often, there were attempts to provide a benevolent spin to colonialism, but these often fell short when the realities were presented.

One of the main purposes of education was to turn African children into people who would yearn for what was the best in British culture or to turn them into anglophiles. Mahatma Gandhi, who had considered himself an Indian and a member of the British Empire, quickly found out when he arrived in South Africa, that racism prevented him from enjoying what was reserved for Whites in South Africa. His education and mannerisms, his knowledge of English law, his craving to serve the British Army during the Zulu War, did not open the doors into the community of Whites in South Africa. He was an anglophile but was not part of the community. Years later, Mandela was to admit that "the educated Englishman was our model; what we aspired to be were "black Englishmen", ... We were taught-and believed-that the best ideas were English ideas, the best government was English government, and the best men were Englishmen," (1994, p. 37). Deculturalization was part of the educational process, and it sought to show African students that British culture was infinitely better, and worth emulating (Armah 2008; Wa Thiongo 2012). Mandela, like many other Africans who underwent British colonial education, experienced the seductive but deceptive nature of that education. Reflecting on his being awarded his undergraduate degree, he observed that he was already on his "way to being drawn into the black elite that Britain sought to create in Africa," (Mandela 1994, p. 97).

5. Racism, Education, and African Children

To a great extent, the struggle for the education of African children in the colonies (as well as in Britain and the United States) was contested at both global and local levels. That is to say, there were people who fought to maintain segregation, and some who fought against it. Although British and United States policies at governmental level tended to support and enforce racism, there were places for contesting both colonialism and racism. As Blacks in Britain and the United States attained education and formal literacy, they formed different associations to champion the causes of Black children. Even the different Pan-Africanism Conferences were initially in Britain, and they brought into focus the challenges Blacks faced at a global level (Killingray 2009).

However, it should be noted that the level of organization that opposed racism and segregation was generally outside the structures of recognized national governments. That is, those who were members of anti-racist or anti-colonial movements rarely came as delegates of either the United States or the British governments. Conversely, it was not uncommon for social scientists and government policy makers to base their decisions on a comparative study of race relations and education (Curry 2009). Frederickson, for example, studied racism in South Africa and the United States. Likewise, those who designed Bantu education or apartheid education in South Africa based their policies on what they had observed in the United States and in Britain. In explaining the mission and purpose of apartheid education, one of its designers, Dr. Verwoerd stated:

> When I am controller of Native Education I will reform it so that the natives will be taught from childhood to realize that equality with Europeans is not for them ... The Bantu must be guided to serve his own community. There is no place for him in the European community above certain forms of labor.... Education must train and teach people in accordance with their opportunities in life-according to the sphere in which they live. (Birley 1968, p. 153, as quoted in Johnson 1982, p. 219)

It becomes apparent then, that one of the primary purposes of educating African children in the colonies was to condition them to accept positions of service and inferiority, based on their race. Addressing legislators in South Africa, the chief administrator of the Transvaal Province pointed out that the South African government "must win the fight against the non-White in the classroom instead of losing it in the battlefield" (, as cited in Johnson 1982, p. 214). Schools often became a battleground for the souls of the nation, and students played a leading role (Molteno 1987). National governments did not hide the fact that they used education to structure and control society, that education was, in a way, a tool for social engineering (Bowles and Gintis 1976; Johnson 1982). This re-engineering of society was based on and designed to teach Africans about the place to which they belonged in relation to Europeans. Education, as it were, was to shape the political, social, cultural, and economic direction of the colonies. Education, in so far as it molded or prepared children for their future roles, reinforced and reproduced racist structures.

A significant number of teachers in the colonies also came from Britain and the United States as well as other European countries (Armah 2008; Johnson 1982). Many of these teachers had also been trained under systems that were based on the racism and racist ideologies of the day. Fully aware of the advantages enjoyed by Europeans in Britain and the United States, such educators argued that "education for whites must fit them to maintain their unquestioned superiority and supremacy" (Johnson 1982, p. 216). One quickly realizes, then, that African and European children in British colonies did not receive the same education: one was taught to serve, the other to rule (Kros 2002). That was how colonial society was envisioned. Expenditures for the education of White students were generally ten times higher than those for Black or African students (Behr and Macmillan 1966).

6. Colonial Curriculum and Social Reproduction

The power of the curriculum to shape the economic, social and political futures of students has been documented by several scholars, (Appel 2004; Armah 1972; Collins 2009; Steans and Tepe 2010). Among those who studied the sociology of education or the curriculum, it became apparent that the curriculum played a huge role in social and economic reproduction. Collins (2009) observed that there was a direct connection between educational experiences, economic life, and ways of living, especially in North America and England. As such, many questioned the idea that education and schooling could bring about social and economic transformation. For Foucault (1984), "Any system of education is a political way of maintaining or modifying the appropriation of discourses, along with the knowledges and powers which they carry" (p. 123, as cited in Christie 1990, p. 37).

Although schooling and education were often marketed as a way for upward mobility, it would appear as if there was an expected limit to how high African students would climb, especially considering the racism that undergirded colonialism. Critical sociologists questioned the veracity of the purposes of the curriculum, observing that "schooling practices, in particular curriculum, pedagogy and evaluation, were themselves related to the unequal patterns of social power" (Christie 1990, p. 37). Over time, African students in British colonies realized the stumbling blocks posed by education (Christie and Collins 1982; Morrow 1990).

For educational sociologists, it was important to understand that "in essence schooling is organized to provide individuated, technical knowledge to select strata of consumer-workers, largely white, middle class, and compliant" (Collins 2009, p. 37). Although Bourdieu and Passeron (1977) and Bowles and Gintis (1976) studied schools in Europe and North America, their observations on education and social reproduction are applicable to the context in colonial Africa, especially given the extent to which European and North American curricula were adapted in Africa. The model of industrial education that was exported to Africa, for example, was based on the education at Tuskegee and the Hampton Institute (Yamada 2008). In addition, it was not uncommon for the American specialist to serve as an expert on educational issues in Africa and the colonies (Persianis 1996; Whitehead 1981). The racial caste system that was prevalent in North America prior to the Civil Rights Act was exported to Africa, with apartheid providing a mirror-image of Plessey vs. Ferguson. Within apartheid:

> A de jure racial hierarchy divided the population into four groups: whites, Indians, coloureds, and black Africans. Rights and benefits were allocated according to this hierarchy, with whites being most advantaged and black Africans being most disadvantaged. As with every aspect of social, political, and economic life under apartheid, education was racially stratified. (Teeger 2015, p. 228)

For the most part, curriculum practices in British colonies were almost consistent, whether it was Ghana (Boampong 2013), Nigeria (Bude 1983), East Africa (Beck 1966), or Southern Africa (Appel 1989; Booth 2003; Brookes 1930). Writing on curriculum and education in South Africa, Christie observed:

> Curriculum control has been an integral part both of the South African education system, and of its contestation. From the State's side apartheid education has always been the strict definition of what State schools and what the organizing principles of the curriculum should be. (Christie 1990, p. 38)

7. The Colonial Curriculum

Granted the emphasis on industrial education that was designed for Africans, the curriculum was largely designed on vocational trades or skills, even from elementary education. In most schools, gardening was part of the curriculum. However, it was mostly the growing of vegetable gardens, rather than flower gardens that was encouraged. Bude (1983) observed that many boarding schools had their own gardens and cash crops. Although the gardens and crops could be used as evidence of the success of industrial education, the produce also helped meet the needs of the students, especially at a time when African schools received very little funding from the government.

Among the main subjects taught to African students included agriculture, poultry, vegetables, orchards, hygiene, first aid, handcrafts, carpentry, home economics, cooking, dressmaking, and, bricklaying (Booth 2003; Bude 1983). Such subjects were designed as part of early vocational training, and in many ways, were meant to prepare African children for the service, manufacturing, and agricultural sectors (Spivey 1978). Different vocational trades were made available to boys, and others to girls, thereby introducing an element of sexism. Girls, for example, were encouraged to study housekeeping, cooking, sewing, and child-care. While the curriculum was designed in Europe and North America, the colonial governments acquiesced:

> It was easy for the colonial powers of Africa to relish a philosophy of education and life that stood for black acquiescence and obedience to the status quo. Tuskegee students-or 'Captains of Industry' as Booker T. Washington liked to call them-were welcome in Colonial Nigeria, the Belgian Congo, South Africa, and throughout British East Africa in the early twentieth century. (Spivey 1978, p. 2)

The access to vocational and/or industrial education was not meant to help Africans succeed or show their skills above their European counterparts (Maylam 2001; Shepherd 1965). The underlying assumption, as far as academic achievement was concerned, was that Africans could not gain mastery in 'bookish subjects.' There was no expectation that Africans would compete for positions with the colonizers.

Even with the emphasis on industrial education, there were occasions when African students were offered an academic curriculum. Among the subjects were English, History, Religious Knowledge, Latin, (African language) Arithmetic, Geometry, Algebra, Geography, Physics, and Chemistry (Omolewa 2006). All these subjects, other than African languages, were taught from a colonial perspective, and for the most part, English was the medium of instruction. Success or passing English language was considered an integral part of being considered successful in the examinations. Because of the academic curriculum's focus on Europe and North America, there was a tendency to portray African countries as traditional and backward, while Europe and North America were viewed as modern and developed.

Extra-curricular activities, including sports, were also segregated, and some were available to European or White students, while others were available to both Africans and European students. The earning potential as a result of playing in those sports, should students want to turn professional, was also very different (Grier 1999). Cricket, rugby, tennis, hockey, and polo were generally for White students. Soccer, netball, volleyball, track and field events, on the other hand, were open to all students, although they had a considerably lower earning potential (Davies 1986).

8. Early Independence: Decolonization and the Rebirth of Indigenous Knowledge

After the attainment of political independence, many former British colonies began to change their educational systems, focusing on nation-building and reconciliation. Almost all the newly independent countries began a process of decolonizing knowledge and education (Ndlovu-Gatsheni 2017). Kenya, a former British colony in East Africa, adopted the policy of Uhuru (Mazrui 1963; Tembe 2013). The emphasis was on helping Kenya develop, especially for populations that had been marginalized, including those in the rural areas. Through the educational philosophy of Uhuru, a new emphasis on human rights and indigenous cultures was encouraged (Mawere 2015; Press 2015).

Tanzania, on the other hand, embarked on Ujamaa, an educational philosophy slightly modeled on socialism, but made to address African or Tanzanian realities, (Ibhawoh and Dibua 2003; Raikes 1975; Schneider 2004). The hope, then, was that socialism would reverse decades of underdevelopment and segregation. Schools and education were envisioned to play a huge role in the development of the nation. However, Ujamaa also assumed a Pan-Africanist dimension, and Tanzania dedicated most of its resources to advancing sub-Saharan countries (Ibhawoh and Dibua 2003).

For South Africa, apartheid was replaced by Masakhane, a philosophy designed to help South Africans work together. Masakhane (let us build each other up) was meant to negate apartheid or segregation (Mandela 1994). Mandela invited South Africans from all racial groups (as well as the international community) to help address the challenges the nation faced as it emerged from colonialism and apartheid.

9. Conclusions

The education of African children in British colonies was problematic, mainly because of a somewhat deceptive nature. It promised advancement and upward social mobility, but in reality, trained them for subordinate roles in societies where racism was legal (Kraak 1991). While African children could yearn to be British (aspiring to be Englishmen, in the words of Nelson Mandela) that avenue was closed to them, especially under apartheid. Reflecting on her education under conditions which privileged racism, in words eerily reminiscent to those of Mandela, Salazar observed:

> In the third grade, I desperately wanted to be White. My teachers privileged whiteness through the English language and U.S. culture, and they excluded all that was native to me; hence, I ascertained that White children were smarter, more attractive, and affluent. As a result, I became a connoisseur of whiteness when I was eight years old. (Salazar 2013, p. 122)

Although colonized by the British and having adopted almost everything that was British (language, religion, sports, politics), African students remained outsiders, even if at times optimistic with regard to the opportunities available through education (Dube 1985; Jansen 1996). Africans who survived British colonial schooling expressed a yearning for a more humanizing education (Hammett and Staeheli 2013). At the same time, they recognize their inability to solve African problems, mainly because colonial education was not designed to make conditions better for Africans. The emphasis on industrial education for African students, however, leaves one pondering: was there more to the purposes of the colonial curriculum which could develop their human potential instead of reducing them to mere laborers? Colonial education, as it were, resulted in the creation or making of a new African, an anglophile whose values were shaped by a new educational system that negated what it was designed to deliver. Under colonialism, every educational system and every colonial institution had, as its purpose, the remolding of the African child.

Author Contributions: T.Q.M.: Conceptualization, Writing, Methodology, Final Paper; M.M.: Conceptualization, Initial Draft, Analysis.

Funding: This research received no external funding.

Conflicts of Interest: The authors declare no conflict of interest.

References

Altheide, David L., and Christopher J. Schneider. 2013. *Qualitative Media Analysis*. Thousand Oaks: Sage, vol. 38.
Appel, Stephen. 1989. Outstanding individuals do not arise from ancestrally poor stock: Racial science and the education of Black South Africans. *The Journal of Negro Education* 58: 544–57.
Appel, Michael. 2004. *Ideology and the Curriculum*. Boston and New York: Routledge.
Armah, Ayi Kwei. 1972. *Why Are We So Blest?* London: Heinemann.
Armah, Ayi Kwei. 2000. *Two Thousand Seasons*. Popenguine: Per Ankh.
Armah, Ayi Kwei. 2008. *Osiris Rising*. Popenguine: Per Ankh.
Armah, Ayi Kwei. 2010. *Remembering the Dismembered Continent*. Popenguine: Per Ankh.
Beck, Ann. 1966. Colonial Policy and Education in British East Africa, 1900–50. *Journal of British Studies* 5: 115–38. [CrossRef]
Behr, Abraham Leslie, and R. G. Macmillan. 1966. *Education in South Africa*. Pretoria: J. L. van Schaik Ltd.
Beittel, Adam. 1951. Some effects of the "Separate but Equal" Doctrine of Education. *The Journal of Negro Education* 20: 140–47. [CrossRef]
Bengtsson, Mariette. 2016. How to plan and perform a qualitative study using content analysis. *NursingPlus Open* 2: 8–14. [CrossRef]
Birley, Robert. 1968. African Education in South Africa. *African Affairs* 67: 152–58. [CrossRef]
Boampong, Cyrelene Amoah. 2013. Rethinking British colonial policy in the Gold Coast: The language factor. *Transactions of the Historical Society of Ghana* 15: 137–57.
Bogdan, Robert, and Sari Knopp Biklen. 2006. *Qualitative Research for Education: An Introduction to Theories and Methods*, 5th ed. Boston: Pearson.

Booth, Zoller Margaret. 2003. Settler, missionary, and the State: Contradictions in the formulation of educational policy in colonial Swaziland. *History of Education* 32: 35–56. [CrossRef]
Bourdieu, Pierre, and Jean-Claude Passeron. 1977. *Reproduction in Education, Society, and Culture*. Beverly Hills: Sage.
Bowen, Glenn A. 2009. Document analysis as a qualitative research method. *Qualitative Research Journal* 9: 27–40. [CrossRef]
Bowles, Samuel, and Herbert Gintis. 1976. *Schooling in Capitalist America*. New York: Basic Books.
Brookes, Edgar. 1930. *Native Education in South Africa*. Pretoria: Van Schaik.
Bude, Udo. 1983. The Adaptation concept in British colonial education. *Comparative Education* 19: 341–55. [CrossRef]
Chisholm, Linda. 1983. Redefining skills: Black Education in South Africa in the 1980s. *Comparative Education* 19: 357–71. [CrossRef]
Christie, Pam. 1990. *The Right to Learn: The Struggle for Education in South Africa*. Cape Town: Ravan Press.
Christie, Pam, and C. Collins. 1982. Bantu education: Apartheid ideology of labour reproduction? *Comparative Education* 18: 59–75. [CrossRef]
Clark, Tom, and Benjamin Lauderdale. 2012. The Genealogy of Law. *Political Analysis* 20: 329–50. [CrossRef]
Collins, James. 2009. Social Reproduction in classrooms and schools. *Annual Review of Anthropology* 38: 33–48. [CrossRef]
Corby, Richard. 1990. Educating Africans for inferiority under British rule: Bo school in Sierra Leone. *Comparative Education Review* 34: 314–49. [CrossRef]
Creswell, John, and Cheryl Poth. 2018. *Qualitative Inquiry and Research Design: Choosing among Five Traditions*. Thousand Oaks: Sage.
Curry, Tommy. 2009. Royce, racism, and the colonial ideal: White Supremacy and the illusion of Civilization in Josiah Royce's account of the White Man's Burden. *The Pluralist* 4: 10–38. [CrossRef]
Davies, John. 1986. Politics, sport and education in South Africa. *African Affairs* 85: 351–63. [CrossRef]
Diop, Cheikh Anta. 1974. *African Origin of Civilization: Myth or Reality*. Chicago: Chicago Review.
Dube, F. 1985. Racism and education in South Africa: The history of European-influenced education in South Africa. *Harvard Education Review* 55: 86–100. [CrossRef]
French, Craig. 2011. Nietzsche, Genealogy and Political Authority. *Polity* 43: 7–35. [CrossRef]
Glesne, Corrine. 2016. *Becoming Qualitative Researchers: An Introduction*, 5th ed. Boston: Pearson.
Grier, Robin. 1999. Colonial legacies and economic growth. *Public Choice* 98: 317–35. [CrossRef]
Hammett, Daniel, and Lynn Staeheli. 2013. Transition and the education of the new South African citizen. *Comparative Education Review* 57: 309–31. [CrossRef]
Hickman, Mary. 1993. Integration or Segregation? The Education of the Irish in Britain in Roman Catholic Voluntary-Aided Schools. *British Journal of Sociology of Education* 14: 285–300. [CrossRef]
Ibhawoh, Bonny, and J. Dibua. 2003. Deconstructing Ujamaa: The Legacy of Julius Nyerere in the Quest for Social and Economic Development in Africa. *African Journal of Political Science/Revue Africaine De Science Politique* 8: 59–83.
Jansen, Jonathan. 1996. Curriculum as a political phenomenon: Historical reflections on Black South African Education. *Journal of Negro Education* 59: 195–206. [CrossRef]
Johnson, Walton. 1982. Education: Keystone of Apartheid. *Anthropology & Education Quarterly* 13: 214–37.
Jones, T. J. 1925. East Africa and education. *The Southern Workman*, June. 239–53.
Killingray, David. 2009. Rights, land, and labour: Black British Critics of South African Policies before 1948. *Journal of Southern African Studies* 35: 375–98. [CrossRef]
Kraak, Andre. 1991. Making the hidden curriculum the formal curriculum: Vocational training in South Africa. *Comparative Education Review* 35: 406–29. [CrossRef]
Kros, Cynthia. 2002. W.W.M. Eiselen: Architect of apartheid education. In *The History of Education under Apartheid 1948–94: The Doors of Learning and Culture Shall Be Opened*. Edited by Peter Kallaway. Cape Town: Pearson.
Loram, Charles Templeman. 1927. *The Education of the South African Native*. London: Longmans Green.
Malisa, Mark. 2010. *(Anti)Narcissisms and (Anti)Capitalisms: Education and Human Nature in Mahatma Gandhi, Malcolm X, Nelson Mandela and Jurgen Habermas*. Boston and Rotterdam: Sense Publishers.
Mandela, Nelson. 1994. *Long Walk to Freedom: The Autobiography of Nelson Mandela*. Boston: Back Bay.
Margo, Robert. 1986. Educational achievement in segregated school systems: The effects of "Separate-but-Equal". *The American Economic Review* 76: 794–801.

Mawere, Munyiaradzi. 2015. Indigenous Knowledge and Public Education in Sub-Saharan Africa. *Africa Spectrum* 50: 57–71. [CrossRef]

Maylam, Paul. 2001. *South Africa's Racial Past: The History and Historiography of Racism, Segregation and Apartheid*. Aldershot: Ashgate.

Mazrui, Ali. 1963. On Heroes and Uhuru-Worship. *Transition* 11: 23–28. [CrossRef]

Molteno, Frank. 1987. Students take control: The 1980 boycott of coloured education in the Cape Peninsular. *British Journal of Sociology of Education* 8: 3–21. [CrossRef]

Morrow, Walter Eugene. 1990. *Aims of Education in South Africa*. New York: Springer.

Ndlovu-Gatsheni, Sabelo. 2017. The Emergence and Trajectories of Struggles for an 'African University': The Case of Unfinished Business of African Epistemic Decolonisation. *Kronos* 43: 51–77. [CrossRef]

O'Leary, Zina. 2014. *The Essential Guide to Doing Your Research Project*, 2nd ed. Thousand Oaks: SAGE Publications, Inc.

Ofori-Attah, Kwabena. 2006. The British and Curriculum development in West Africa: A Historical discourse. *International Review of Education* 52: 409–23. [CrossRef]

Omolewa, Michael. 2006. Educating the "Native": A Study of the Education Adaptation Strategy in British Colonial Africa, 1910–36. *The Journal of African American History* 91: 267–87. [CrossRef]

Onderwysblad, July 1.

Paterson, Andrew. 2005. "The Gospel of Work Does Not Save Souls": Conceptions of industrial and agricultural education for Africans in the Cape Colony, 1890–930. *History of Education Quarterly* 45: 377–404. [CrossRef]

Patton, Michael. 2015. *Qualitative Research & Evaluation Methods*. Thousand Oaks: Sage.

Persianis, Panayiotis. 1996. The British colonial education 'Lending' Policy in Cyprus (1878–1960): An intriguing example of an elusive 'Adapted Education' policy. *Comparative Education* 32: 45–68. [CrossRef]

Pinar, William, and Charles Bowers. 1992. Politics of Curriculum: Origins, Controversies, and Significance of Critical Perspectives. *Review of Research in Education* 18: 163–90. [CrossRef]

Press, Robert Maxwell. 2015. Establishing a Culture of Resistance. In *Ripples of Hope: How Ordinary People Resist Repression Without Violence*. Amsterdam: Amsterdam University Press, pp. 233–64.

Raikes, Phillip Lawrence. 1975. Ujamaa and Rural Socialism. *Review of African Political Economy* 2: 33–52. [CrossRef]

Roberts, A. 1905. *South African Native Affairs Commission*. Cape Town: Cape Times, vol. 2.

Roche, John. 1951. The Future of "Separate but Equal". *Phylon (1940–1956)* 12: 219–26. [CrossRef]

Salazar, Maria del Carmen. 2013. A Humanizing pedagogy: Reinventing the principles and practice of education as a journey toward liberation. *Review of Research in Education* 37: 121–48. [CrossRef]

Schensul, Stephen, Jean Schensul, and Margaret LeCompte. 1999. *Essential Ethnographic Methods: Observations, Interview, and Questionnaires: Vol 2. Ethnographer's Toolkit*. Walnut Creek: AltaMira.

Schneider, Leander. 2004. Freedom and Unfreedom in Rural Development: Julius Nyerere, Ujamaa Vijijini, and Villagization. *Canadian Journal of African Studies* 38: 344–92.

Shepherd, R. 1965. The South African Bantu Education Act. *African Affairs* 54: 138–42. [CrossRef]

Spivey, Donald. 1978. The African crusade for Black industrial schooling. *The Journal of Negro History* 63: 1–17. [CrossRef]

Steans, Jill, and Daniela Tepe. 2010. Introduction—Social reproduction in international political economy: Theoretical insights and international, transnational and local settings. *Review of International Political Economy* 17: 807–15. [CrossRef]

Sutton, Jane, and Zubin Austin. 2015. Qualitative research: Data collection, analysis, and management. *The Canadian Journal of Hospital Pharmacy* 68: 226–31. [CrossRef] [PubMed]

Teeger, Chana. 2015. Ruptures in the Rainbow Nation: How desegregated South African schools deal with interpersonal and structural racism. *Sociology of Education* 88: 226–43. [CrossRef]

Tembe, Joel Das Neves. 2013. Uhuru na Kazi: Recapturing MANU Nationalism through the Archive. *Kronos* 39: 257–79.

Thomas, Jerry, Jack Nelson, and Stephen Silverman. 2015. *Research Methods in Physical Activity*, 7th ed. Champaign: Human Kinetics.

Vucetic, Srdjan. 2011. Genealogy as a research tool in International Relations. *Review of International Studies* 37: 1295–312. [CrossRef]

Wa Thiongo, Ngugi. 2008. *The River Between*. Boston and London: Pearson.

Wa Thiongo, Ngugi. 2012. *Decolonizing the Mind*. Harare: Zimbabwe Publishing House, Heinemann.

Wa Thiongo, Ngugi. 2014. *Globaletics: Theory and the Politics of Knowing*. New York: Columbia University Press.

Walker, Vanessa Siddle, and Kim Nesta Archung. 2003. The Segregated schooling of Blacks in the Southern United States and South Africa. *Comparative Education Review* 47: 21–40. [CrossRef]

Whitehead, Clive. 1981. Education in British Colonial Dependencies, 1919–39: A Re-Appraisal. *Comparative Education* 17: 71–80. [CrossRef]

Yamada, Shoko. 2008. Educational borrowing as negotiation: Re-examining the influence of the American Black industrial education model on British colonial education in Africa. *Comparative Education* 44: 21–37. [CrossRef]

© 2019 by the authors. Licensee MDPI, Basel, Switzerland. This article is an open access article distributed under the terms and conditions of the Creative Commons Attribution (CC BY) license (http://creativecommons.org/licenses/by/4.0/).

Article

Younger Infants in the Elementary School: Discursively Constructing the Under-Fives in Institutional Spaces and Practices

Yinka Olusoga

Carnegie School of Education, Leeds Beckett University, Headingley Campus, Leeds LS6 3QQ, UK; Y.Olusoga@leedsbeckett.ac.uk

Received: 6 May 2019; Accepted: 5 July 2019; Published: 9 July 2019

Abstract: Expansion of state-regulation of education and care for under-fives in England has seen increasing numbers of under-fives attending primary school early years provision in the 21st century's opening decades. However, this is not entirely novel as under-fives attending elementary school feature in numerous 19th and 20th century reports. This article examines how under-fives have been discursively constructed in three reports between 1861 and 1933. Changing conceptualizations of under-fives are reflected in these documents. Shifting discourses of schooling, child development and curriculum are deployed, adapted or silenced to frame and judge the personal, social and moral conduct of the young child and parent. This normalizing discursive gaze positions the spaces and practices of schooling as necessary interventions inculcating specific governmentally designated desirable aspects of the child. Under-fives are enmeshed in an advancing process of educational colonization that removes them from the home, coming to dominate their time and experiences as young children. Current trends towards earlier school starting ages, longer daily hours, and the forensic use of data to chart progress towards expected goals is extension of this pattern. Attending to the genealogy of the discursive rationalization of this process helps us to critique how similar contemporary policy arguments are made.

Keywords: under-fives in elementary schools; purposes of nursery schooling; schooling for parental responsibility; maternal duties; school readiness

1. Introduction

For more than 150 years, the early care and education of young children in England has been a focus of official policy discussion. From the Report of the Newcastle Commission in 1861 (Education Commission 1861a), to ongoing debates in the 2010s (Gibb et al. 2010; Office for Standards in Education Ofsted), the status and treatment of children under five in state-funded school provision has been a focus for educational, social political attention. The desirability of including or excluding under-fives from state-funded school provision has been shaped at different points in time by a range of competing, overlapping and contradictory discourses (Palmer 2011; Read 2015). These discourses are informed by ideas about the role of the parent (especially of the mother), of the role the state and its institutions, and about the nature of children. What is notable in these discourses is the intersection between social class and gender and a tendency for the needs of the child to be constructed in terms of the needs of the system, of society and of the economy. This article will examine three historical reports that address the issue of under-fives in what was originally termed elementary education. They are the Report of the Newcastle Commission (Education Commission 1861a), the Report of the Consultative Committee upon the School Attendance of Children Below the Age of Five (Board of Education 1908), and the Hadow Report on Infant and Nursery Schools (Board of Education 1933). Finally, this article will reflect on changes and continuities in these constructions across these documents and into contemporary (at the time of writing) policy debates.

2. Method

The theoretical frame for engagement with these texts draws on Foucault's work on discourse and on genealogy (Foucault 1970, 1972). It employs an understanding of discourse as productive. Discourse does not merely describe what already exists; it produces habitual linguistic practices that name, construct and act on people and groups as objects of knowledge to be classified and sorted. Furthermore, Foucault's concept of genealogy identifies how power and knowledge are fused. His concept of Power/Knowledge allows analysis of the social and material consequences of discourse. These consequences can be traced in the debates and reports on the care and education of young children and in the accompanying development of dividing, disciplinary practices that classify and sort children and families. Application of Foucault's ideas helps this study to uncover the growth and development of nurseries and schools as institutions of surveillance that bring increasing numbers of children and families and under their normalizing gaze (Foucault 1977). The analysis of the historical texts under scrutiny focuses on how under-fives, their parents and homes, and institutions for their care and education outside the home are discursively constructed at these earlier points in time in the 19th and 20th centuries. Informed by the discourse-historical approach to critical discourse analysis (Reisigl and Wodak 2016), this discursive construction is traced by considering the ways language is used to name and characterize children, parents, homes and provision in the historical reports under examination. The focus texts have been read and re-read iteratively to facilitate an analysis of the nature of the arguments employed in this naming and characterizing, noting on which grounds they are predicated. These multiple readings also take note of whose perspectives are taken, who is written about and whose views are represented, whose ignored or undermined, and how language is used to intensify or mitigate the arguments presented in the texts.

3. Infants Schools versus Dames' Schools: Discursively Constructing Schools for Children in Infancy in 1861

3.1. The Royal Commission on Popular Education, 1861

Nine years before state education became compulsory for children aged between five and 10 in England and Wales, the Newcastle Commission was asked to enquire into the state of popular education and to consider whether it needed to be extended. State involvement and funding of education for the working classes was a highly contentious issue, with some arguing for the development of a proper national system of state-supported education, and others deeply opposed to the idea (Aldrich 2006). To discharge this task, the Commission, via the work of its Assistant Commissioners, conducted a survey of nine specimen regions of the country. This involved visiting schools, talking with school managers and gathering evidence from those who dealt with the working classes in a range of fields including employment, policing, and religion. In addition, the Commissioners sent out a circular of questions, selected and called expert witnesses, collated and surveyed decades of official statistics and reports on education and related issues and commissioned reports on the situation in other countries. The result of their work was published in 1861 in a six-volume report. Volume I of the Report examined the range of types of schooling available to the mass of the independent poor (by which it meant those able to earn a living rather than being reliant on indoor or outdoor poor relief), as well as that provided for pauper children and children they classed as 'vagrants and criminals' (Education Commission 1861a, p. 386).

For 'children above infancy' who came from families classed as the independent poor, the Report discussed day (elementary) schools, evening schools and Sunday schools (Education Commission 1861a, p. 28). For younger children, it discussed the infant school, a category it sub-divided into 'the private or dames' schools' and 'the public infant schools' (Education Commission 1861a). So-called

Dame Schools had existed for centuries and were a popular option for families of all respectable classes, but many issues had been raised about these, including variable quality and the fact that some operated purely as a minding service, were often managed by very elderly women, and due to lack of regulation, could put children in danger due to over-crowding. Infant schools, on the other hand, tended to be departments of existing day schools, regulated and inspected by the state. It was in these discussions that the working-class parent and home were discursively constructed, and the working-class child characterized as in need of early intervention in state-approved institutions for its care and instruction.

3.2. The Working-Class Parent and the Need for Schools for Children in Infancy

The Report stated that infant schools provided:

> the sort of instruction which in the wealthier classes of society is conveyed almost imperceptibly by constant intercourse with educated persons. (Education Commission 1861a, p. 28)

By contrast, the Report's view of the interactions between working-class parents and their children was one that stressed their presumed ignorance, lack of resources and the consuming nature of their economic and domestic labor:

> In the family of a mechanic or day labourer, to say nothing of the ignorance of the parents, the father is usually at work from six in the morning till six at night. The mother has to perform personally all household operations. Stationery and books are too valuable to be made into toys. The house is not furnished with objects which awaken intelligence, nor has anyone leisure to form the manners and temper of the child. (Education Commission 1861a, p. 28)

In line with practices in other comparable counties such as Germany, France and America, in the 1860s the nominal starting age for most day school provision in England and Wales was six or seven. However, the Report found that children attended infant schools 'from the very earliest age at which they are able to walk alone and to speak' (Education Commission 1861a, p. 28). The Report positioned the infant school as the solution to practical and social problems associated with the containment of the very young. Infant schools were described as:

> the only means of keeping the children of such families out of the streets in towns, or out of the roads and fields in the country. (Education Commission 1861a, p. 28)

Thus, very young children were characterized as both in potential danger and as a potential threat to the functioning of public spaces. The Report considered the educational worth of the infant school lay not in the amount of knowledge that very young children gained (acknowledged as 'apparently small in amount' but 'of high value'), but in its ability to instill 'habits of docility and submission to discipline' (Education Commission 1861a, p. 28).

3.3. The Dames' Schools versus the Infant Schools

Having established this role for infant schools, the Report compared the dames' schools and the government-inspected public infant schools. At the heart of the discussion was an ideological tension between the concepts of care and of education, and between provision for the young child that mimicked the atmosphere of the home and institutional provision that reflected the roles and practices of schooling. The descriptions of the dames' schools contained some of the most striking and emotive language in the entire Report. The uninspected, domestic and feminine aspects of the provision were construed as highly problematic. Dames' schools were dismissed as being 'little more than nurseries run by women generally advanced in life' (Education Commission 1861a, p. 29) who looked after children from their local communities. The Report stated:

> their school is usually their kitchen, sitting and bed-room and the scene of all their domestic occupations. (Education Commission 1861a, p. 29)

It described how dames' schools were 'apt to be close, crowded, and dirty' with an atmosphere so 'oppressive' as to make a visitor feel sick (Education Commission 1861a, p. 29). Against this was contrasted the public infant school, characterized and positioned as a far preferable, clinical and institutional space.

3.4. The Purpose and Outcomes of Schooling for the Working-Class Infant

The distinctive look and feel of the public infant school were emphasized in the Report. Public infant schools, it stated presented a 'different appearance' as a result of the 'attention ... bestowed upon their organization'. Further distinction was made with the claim that, unlike the dames' schools they:

> not only aim at, but in fact accomplish, a great deal more than the simple objective of keeping children out of mischief. (Education Commission 1861a, pp. 29–30)

The Report outlined the educational approach of the public infant school in some detail and discursively characterized the young child in terms of its ability to engage in different types of educational activity. Divided into two classes, the youngest children (i.e., the under-fives) in such schools engaged in activities to promote talking, develop their physical skills and to learn 'their letters' (Education Commission 1861a, p. 30). The older infant children in the higher division were told stories, including bible stories, learned basic arithmetic using suitable equipment and were 'exercised in plaiting, tying knots, sewing, and other occupations which employ their hands' (Education Commission 1861a, p. 30). This instruction was deemed to demand a teacher with 'tact, patience, and ingenuity' with a 'special taste for the occupation' (Education Commission 1861a, p. 30).

An emphasis on the need for the social and moral training of children, in ways that they would come to embody, was reflected in the statement that:

> Churches are good, and ordinary schools are good, but they only modify bad habits already contracted. Infant schools prevent bad habits been formed. (Education Commission 1861a, p. 31)

The very young children of the poor were thus discursively framed as in need of a program of moral inculcation that would instill in them habits of thought and action and reduce time spent in the contaminating influence of home. The outcome of such instruction was physically and socially evident in the children, who received in the public infant schools:

> training in obedience, attention, observation, and facility of comprehension, which distinguishes them at a glance from children who have not had the advantage of an infant school training. (Education Commission 1861a, p. 31)

Finally, the Newcastle Commission Report drew on the testimony of Mr. Shields, a London headmaster called before the Commissioners as an expert witness. He argued that an extension of government support to develop public infant school provision would facilitate careful preparation of young children. In his evidence he stated that he would admit children into the infant class of his day school 'as soon as they could be brought' and keep them 'as a rule till they are seven years of age' (Education Commission 1861b, p. 531). This he argued could essentially speed up the process of educating them in the day schools from age seven so that they could 'thoroughly well all the absolute essentials of education by 11 years of age' (Education Commission 1861a, p. 31).

Although the Report of the Newcastle Commission did not immediately lead to the establishment of a national system of education, it did prove to be highly influential in shaping the debates in parliament that resulted in the 1870 Elementary Education (Foster) Act. The decision in 1870 to set the school starting age at five drew on the same economic arguments and the same logic of starting educational instruction early (House of Commons Debate, 1870). The dim official view of the dames' schools and the preference for institutional rather than homelike spaces for very young children meant that by the turn of the 20th century local school boards allowed children under five to attend public elementary schools, often in buildings and with equipment poorly suited to their needs.

4. Public Elementary Schools versus Nursery Schools: Discursively Constructing Provision for Under-Fives in 1908

In April 1907, the Consultative Committee had been charged by the Board of Education to provide advice:

> in regard to the desirability, or otherwise, both on educational and other grounds, of discouraging the attendance at school of children under the age of (say) five years. (Board of Education 1908, p. 11)

The eventual report, published in 1908, largely took up the themes established in an earlier report on the same subject by the women inspectors in 1905. That report had argued that where children came from 'good homes' run by 'careful mothers', attendance at elementary school under the age of five was both unnecessary and unnatural (Board of Education 1905b, p. ii). The subsequent Elementary Code for 1905 issued by the Board of Education reflected this and included an amendment to Article 53 which gave Local Education Authorities (LEAs) the right to refuse admission to school of children under five (Board of Education 1905a, p. 21). In cases, however, of children with working mothers or from what they termed 'imperfect homes' they were, in the words of Katherine Bathurst, one of the most critical of the women inspectors, being 'sacrificed ... to the selfishness of their overworked mothers' (Board of Education 1905b, p. 75). In these circumstances the Report recommended that attendance at school was preferable to staying at home. However, they warned against formal approaches to teaching very young children and of the impact of unsuitable furniture and resources on their physical and intellectual development. In the preface to the Report, the Chief Inspector, Cyril Jackson argued that the women inspectors had agreed unanimously that there was 'no intellectual advantage from school instruction' (Board of Education 1905b, p. i), a claim that Read (2015) argues did not capture the nuance of their argument about the failings of unsuitable provision but also of the potential of appropriate pedagogic approaches. The preface continued, stating:

> It would seem that a new form of school is necessary for poor children. The better parents should be discouraged from sending the children before five, while the poorer who must do so, should send them to nursery schools rather than the schools of instruction. (Board of Education 1905b, p. ii)

Attendance at elementary schools of under-fives was a still a pressing question two years later when the Board of Education commissioned the second report on the issue, this time provided by the new Consultative Committee on Education. Despite LEA powers granted in 1905 to refuse admission to children under the age of five 'at least a third' of children between the ages of three and five were registered at public elementary schools (Board of Education 1908, pp. 11–12). Furthermore, little had been provided in the way of nursery provision in light of the 1905 recommendation. The debate on the issue of very young children was positioned in the 1908 Report as partly a medical issue. The first set of witnesses listed in the report were new medical officers, and the report discussed concerns around the stunting the physical and intellectual development of young children and their potential exposure to disease in large, overcrowded classrooms and schools. However, in the bulk of the Report, the school attendance of under-fives was framed as a social issue. Drawing on discourses of social class, gender and eugenics (Read 2015), the issue was argued as arising primarily from a failure of working-class families to provide decent homes and of working-class mothers in particular to provide adequate parenting.

4.1. 'Imperfect Homes': Maternal Duty and Poverty

The 1908 Report stressed, as the 1905 Report had, that the ideal place for young children was the home and that alternative provision was only necessary in cases when the home conditions fell below a certain standard. Discussion of 'imperfect' homes focused on the need for each mother to do 'her duty by her children' (Board of Education 1908, p. 16). Proper maternal duty towards working-class children, according to the Report, involved a mother knowing 'how to care for them properly and to make the best use of her narrow means' (Board of Education 1908, p. 16). Additionally, it meant avoiding employment that would 'keep her out of the home', as well as keeping the home 'clean, well-lighted, well-ventilated, and not over-cramped' with a 'safe space' for the child to play outdoors (Board of Education 1908, p. 16). The 'natural relationship between mother and child' and 'the other influences of good home life', the report argued, represented 'a moral and educational power' (Board of Education 1908, p. 16). Furthermore, this power was one of:

> high national importance to preserve and to strengthen, . . . which educational policy should be careful not to impair. (Board of Education 1908, p. 16)

Thus, the need for women to perform their maternal duty was framed as a form of good citizenship, and a moral duty to the nation, not just to the child. This maternalistic discourse (Read 2015) was informed by the prevalent eugenic discourse (Heathorn 2000; Hendrick 1997), in which children were viewed as genetic stock to be tended by mothers and on whom the health, vigour and progress of the nation depended.

State supported care or educational provision for all under-fives was positioned in the Report as a potential threat to the natural role of the mother and development of the child and to the natural place of women in the home rather than in the workplace. The Report, however, acknowledged that as well as there being some parents 'not sufficiently alive to the well-being of their children' to provide these ideal home conditions, there were also 'many mothers . . . anxious to do their whole duty towards their children' but who were 'unable to train them [the children] properly owing to various circumstances' (Board of Education 1908, pp. 16–17). Such circumstances included lacking 'the necessary means or accommodation' or being 'compelled to leave home during the day and go to work' (Board of Education 1908, p. 17). Poverty and economic disadvantage were thus alluded to, however the Report firmly stated that it was outside 'the province of the Committee to suggest how these difficulties may be overcome' (Board of Education 1908, p. 17). The Report argued that improved 'educational opportunities' would contribute to a:

> steady decrease in the number of those homes in which little children fail to receive the inestimable advantage of right parental care. (Board of Education 1908, p. 19)

Thus, instead of acknowledging societal and structural forces impacting on the ability of families in poverty to provide for their children and to make choices about their care, the focus of the Report remained one that individualized families in poverty and blamed mothers for the existence of these imperfect homes. It positioned education as the means for improving behaviour of the very poor, both as very young children and eventually as parents, without acknowledging any need to address the structural causes of poverty.

4.2. 'Minders', Crèches and Nursery Schools: Care and/or Education for Under-Fives

Having side-stepped discussion of the wider causes of imperfect homes, the Report considered the alternatives available to mothers (not parents) seeking care and/or education for their children under five. Leaving children unattended inside or outside the home was, obviously, dismissed as an option. Leaving children with a neighbor came under the same restrictions as staying with the mother, as neighboring homes were likely to be imperfect for similar reasons. Echoing the findings of the Newcastle Commission of 1861, the 1908 Report took a vociferously dim view of unofficial and non-institutional provision. The Report stated that the 'professional 'minder' is almost always unsatisfactory' (Board of Education 1908, p. 18). Lamenting that the lack of centralized inspection and control over such provision, the Report described minders as 'ignorant women' and their homes as 'dirty and insanitary', and stated:

> It is a well-proved fact that it is a common practice in such places for children to be drugged in order to keep them quiet. (Board of Education 1908, p. 18)

Against this domestic, community-based unofficial provision the Report contrasted institution-based provision for under-fives. The Report named the crèche and the Infant School as institutions catering for under-fives, the essential difference between the two being the educational focus of the Infant School, which was absent from crèche provision. Having identified the existence of crèches, supported via voluntary charities and the award of local government grants in some areas, they, and the children who attended them, were not the main focus of the Report. Instead, attention was paid to discussing the pros and cons of the Infant School. The Committee was keen to stress that infant schools differed widely and that concerns about the general attendance of under-fives in public elementary schools could be allayed by the development of the right sort of infant school provision. Echoing the earlier concerns of the women inspectors, the Report stated that putting young children 'under formal instruction and discipline' (Board of Education 1908, p. 19) as was the case in the infant departments of some Public Elementary Schools, was not good practice. At the other end of the spectrum, however, it identified nursery and infant school provision that was designed to acknowledge and address the specific needs of the very young. Here, the Report stated:

> the special needs of small children are met by the provision of special rooms, special curriculum and special teaching. (Board of Education 1908, p. 19)

Expanding on this discussion the Report set out its description of the 'characteristics of the ideal institution for younger infants' (Board of Education 1908, p. 20). That institution was the nursery school and the Report very much championed its cause. In so doing, it also discursively constructed the particular child for whom such provision was in the Committee's view necessary; the type of teacher suited to the task and the projected outcomes of the child's nursery school experience.

4.3. Describing the Younger Infant: Characteristics and Needs

The 1908 Report devoted attention to considering the particular characteristics of younger infants as a means of justifying a need for distinct provision designed to meet their needs. They were described in the Report as being 'even more dependent on light, air and sunshine than older children' (Board of Education 1908, p. 20). They thus required easy access to a partially covered playground that could accommodate them in all weathers in which, ideally, they should 'spend half the day' (Board of Education 1908, p. 20). Indoors they required classrooms with 'much more floor space' due to their 'natural instinct for movement' (Board of Education 1908, pp. 20–21). Furniture needed to be flexible and moveable to accommodate change and children should be provided with space to sleep, preferably 'in the open-air under proper conditions' (Board of Education 1908, p. 22). Formal lessons in the three Rs 'should be rigidly excluded' and 'no inspection or examination of results in such subjects allowed' (Board of Education 1908, p. 21). Instead, children should engage in a range of hands-on activities, including engaging with Froebelian 'Kindergarten gifts' and in story-telling, drama and other activities to develop their talking and listening (Board of Education 1908, p. 21). In addition:

> Cleanly habits and ready obedience should be secured by a discipline which is kindly, but not unduly repressive. (Board of Education 1908, p. 21)

4.4. Advantages of Nursery School: Moral, Physical and Mental

The justification for the nursery school was further enhanced in the Report by a section examining the advantages younger children would gain from attending such nursery schools. The advantages were classified as being moral, physical and mental. The primacy of moral advantages in the list reflected the argument that such provision should only be aimed at children from the economic and social margins of the working-classes and was predicated on a Malthusian discourse that linked immorality and poverty (Cremaschi 2014). According to this discourse, these were families whose poverty and imperfect homes were signs of an intergenerational moral contamination that schooling must seek to address. The moral advantages listed focused on the role of early schooling in physically containing and morally treating under-fives from such families, allowing them to learn 'important lessons which more fortunately placed children learn at that age in their homes' (Board of Education 1908, p. 24). Nursery schools could keep such children 'away from the dangers and temptations of the streets', instead offering 'cleaner and more wholesome surroundings' than their homes could provide (Board of Education 1908, p. 24). Furthermore, there was a surveillance element as such provision kept the children 'under the eye of a teacher whose influence should be all for the good', where they could be taught:

> to be truthful, kindly, and honest; to be cleanly and tidy in their persons; to be disciplined and obedient in their habits. (Board of Education 1908, p. 24)

The physical advantages outlined in the Report also had a moral aspect and widened surveillance to cover the parents and the mother in particular. School, and the structure that it imposed on family life in relation to time-keeping, meals, clothing and cleanliness, the Report stated, tended 'to improve the physical development of the child' (Board of Education 1908, p. 25). Close observation of this physical development also increased opportunities for teachers and medical staff to detect in children 'diseases and weaknesses, such as defects of sight and hearing' (Board of Education 1908, p. 25). The alleged mental advantages of the infant school were less clearly stated. The Report acknowledged the concerns of some that early attendance at school could lead to the minds of the child becoming 'dulled and injured by being overworked' (Board of Education 1908, p. 25). However, it argued that this would be avoided in provision that followed the 'general nature and function' (Board of Education 1908, p. 25) of the ideal nursery school that had been outlined by the Committee.

4.5. Constructing the Nursery School as a Site of Surveillance

From this discussion of the advantages of nursery schools for under-fives from imperfect homes, a key theme is one of surveillance, both the child and the parent, and especially of the mother. Attendance of a specific class of working-class child in the nursery school could facilitate their early physical surveillance under the normalizing gaze (Foucault 1977) of schooling. This could operate alongside a social surveillance of their behavior and of their capacity for obedience. Nursery schools, as proposed by the Committee, could monitor and mold the child's behavior, but also the quality of parenting. Judgements made against criteria of focused on the child's physical appearance were in effect also proxy measurements of the performance of respectability by the mother in submitting to the specific requirements of school attendance, punctuality, dress and cleanliness. The Report addressed the concern that some would perceive the provision of nursery schools are relieving some of the burden of parental responsibility 'to the moral detriment' of the child and parent (Board of Education 1908, p. 26). Instead, the Committee argued, this provision, targeted at specific homes and families, would actually have the opposite effect:

> in the case of the children under consideration their attendance at school might be a useful means of bringing home to their mothers a livelier sense of their parental duties. (Board of Education 1908, p. 26)

Publicly-funded nursery schools, the Committee argued, should be provided under the discretion of the LEA, for under-fives coming from imperfect homes. Organizationally they should be attached to Public Elementary Schools and ideally be open for the same hours to facilitate children being taken to school by or with older siblings (Board of Education 1908, p. 22). As the Nursery School would, unlike the professional minder or non-educational crèche, offer 'something more than mere nursing' it would come 'under the supervision' of the LEA and would employ 'special methods' and offer the children 'training' that was 'in the proper sense, educational' (Board of Education 1908, p. 53). As well as benefitting from this educational training, the transfer of children at the end of their time in nursery to the infant department would be facilitated by them having 'already been grouped in classes' which would make it 'easier to arrange for their preparation for the classes in the upper school' (Board of Education 1908, p. 53). Thus, despite the Report's eschewing of formal teaching practices for the under-fives, there was a role for the nursery in institutionalizing and preparing the children for the demands and practices of the next phase of their education.

As was the case with the 1861 Report of the Newcastle Commission, the impact of the 1908 Report of the Consultative Committee was not immediate. However, Article 19 of the 1918 Education Act did finally give LEAs the power to provide publicly-funded nursery schools or nursery classes for three to five-year-olds. This was the socially targeted provision the 1908 Report had argued for, aimed children for whom attendance was deemed 'necessary or desirable for their heathy physical and mental development' and the provision was to attend to the children's 'health, nourishment, and physical welfare' (Great Britain 1918, 8 & 9 Geo. 5). The resultant provision also had to be open to inspection by the LEA. Take up of the powers of the Act, however, was limited and geographically uneven.

5. Under-Fives in Nursery Schools and Nursery Classes in 1933

5.1. The 1933 Report on Infant and Nursery Schools

The 1933 Report of the Consultative Committee on Infant and Nursery Schools was the last in a trio of reports focusing on the various stages of the education system (secondary, primary, and finally infant and nursery). Twenty-five years on from the 1908 Report discussed above, the trend was for infant provision to be in schools or departments separate from junior provision. Nursery schools offered provision from age two, targeted at children living in slum conditions, at the discretion of the local authority, nursery classes within infant school took children from the age of three. Only 30 separate nursery schools had been established by LEAs, with a further 25 run by voluntary bodies (Board of Education 1933, p. xv). Therefore, the majority of children receiving state funded nursery provision did so in nursery classes in primary schools, attending the nursery classes between the ages of three and five and the infant classes from five to age seven (Board of Education 1933).

From the beginning the tone and language of the Report strikingly reflected educational, psychological and medical discourses of child development that were international in scope. Key educational theorists and researchers such as Dewey, Montessori and Isaacs were named, and a focus on the supervision and measurement of children's growth and development informed the discussion. Since the turn of the 20th century, the proportion of children under-five attending elementary schools had dropped from a high of 43% in 1900 to 13% in 1930 (Board of Education 1933, p. xv). However, an English tradition of nursery provision and practice had developed, and the Report cited Rachel and Margaret McMillan's outdoor nursery in Deptford (Board of Education 1933, p. 101) and quoted from Grace Owen's 1930 pamphlet 'Education and Nursery Schools' (Board of Education 1933, p. 102). This tradition placed an emphasis on outdoor play, on regular medical supervision focused on physical development and health, and on social training (Read 2015). In line with the exhortations of the women inspectors in 1905, the Report argued that formal approaches to instruction were not part of this nursery tradition. All of this was reflected in the Report's description of the ideal nursery school which:

> should not be 'institutional' in character, but as far as possible of a light and open 'garden pavillion' type. It will consist of a number of class (or play) rooms, rooms for the staff, a room for observation and medical treatment, a kitchen, lavatories and offices. The ideal school is the light single-storey building of the open-air type set in a garden playground; the playground is centrally placed between the classrooms. (Board of Education 1933, p. 169)

5.2. The Aims, Functions and Outcomes of Nursery Provision

In the Report, the Committee reviewed the aims and function of nursery schooling under three headings; namely, the 'medical or hygienic aspect', the 'educational aspect' and the 'social aspect' (Board of Education 1933, p.103). The section of the Report outlining the educational aspect of the nursery school was very brief and emphasized the role of play, rather than formal instruction in children's learning. The section that addressed the medical aspect outlined how nursery provision had become part of the state machinery for medical surveillance of young children that had been recommended in the 1908 Report. Nursery school practice included:

> inspections by the school doctor not less than once a term and sometimes once a month; frequent visits by the school nurse; the systematic measuring and weighing of the children; the exercise of great care in the detection and isolation of cases of infectious illness; and the keeping of a medical record for each child. (Board of Education 1933, p. 104)

The Report thus identified and characterized the under-fives from poor homes who attended nursery schools as children whose physical health was under particular threat in their inadequate homes and communities. Nursery school therefore was positioned as providing the constant medical surveillance and necessary space and facilities for their physical development and training.

The social aspect of nursery schools addressed the personal and social conduct of the child and, potentially, of the parents, characterizing both as in need of intervention. The impact of a poor home environment on children's personal and social development was discussed in the Report in psychological rather than purely moral terms, reflecting changing discourses of education in which both nature and nurture were implicated. The Report stated that 'most psychologists' contended that the mental development of very young children was 'to a large extent determined by specific tendencies which are inherited' (Board of Education 1933, p. 75). In addition, however, the child's early environment played a part and the Committee argued:

> Most causes of moral abnormality and perversion, of nervous disorder and faulty habit-formation, have their roots in these initial years of life. (Board of Education 1933, p. 118)

Attendance at nursery school afforded a compensatory training of 'the child in right personal and social behaviour', via the influence of 'companions of his [sic] own age' and 'sympathetic adults who are able to train him in good habits' (Board of Education 1933, p. 105). Thus, the nursery child could be prepared to become 'a useful member of the community' (Board of Education 1933, p. 105).

5.3. Nursery Provision and the Development of Parental Responsibility

A theme of the 1908 Report had been parental concern that nursery provision could further undermine the responsibility of parents who were judged as providing imperfect homes for their children. In 1933, however, the Committee were clear in their view that nursery school was able to increase feelings and capacities for parental responsibilities in the families targeted by the provision. The Report argued that nursery schools were able to exert 'through the child an influence for good on the standards and ideals of the home' (Board of Education 1933, p. 105). This influence was fostered by the establishment by nursery schools of 'mothers' clubs or guilds' (Board of Education 1933, p. 105). The Report stated:

> Directly or indirectly the mothers gain through these organisations fuller knowledge of their children's needs and possibilities. (Board of Education 1933, p. 105)

Open days, where parents were invited as 'interested spectators of the daily round of school activities' (Board of Education 1933, p. 105), were also cited as means of extending influence of the nursery to the home and of enlisting parents to contribute to the provision in specific, gendered ways:

> The gratitude of the parents is displayed in many ways, for instance mothers help in washing school linen and overalls, and fathers construct toys, and attend to the garden. The sense of parental responsibility is increased, rather than diminished by the attendance of young children at the nursery school. (Board of Education 1933, p. 105)

This discourse on poor working-class parents reflects an intersection of social class and gender. The parents were to be instructed and trained, their poverty taken as proof of their lack of knowledge and inability to be the force for good their children required. They were required to work in partnership with nursery and its staff, but this was a partnership where they watched, learned and followed the instructions given to them. Proof of the impact of the positive influence exerted on them by the nursery was in their practical, gendered performance of gratitude via their gendered labour.

5.4. The Limitations of Nursery Provision

The 1933 Report reiterated the argument presented in 1908 regarding the social need for targeted nursery provision. Nursery schools and classes were, it argued:

> a remedial agency affording partial compensation for unfavourable home environment, and should therefore be provided first in districts where home conditions are bad. (Board of Education 1933, p. 112)

The 1908 Report had maintained a silence on the wider social, economic and political context, that effectively served to individualize and blame parents as the sole cause of their poverty and imperfect homes. The 1933 Report still positioned the correct performance of motherhood as the essential factor in the child's life. Indeed, it argued that 'systematic efforts' in the primary school curriculum 'to give the older girls some instruction in house craft and infant care' (Board of Education 1933, p. 113) would in time decrease the number of children living in inadequate homes. The Committee, however, also argued that the 'problem of the physical and mental welfare' of under-fives was 'essentially sociological' (Board of Education 1933, p. 186) and that action outside of the sphere of early childhood education and care was necessary to make any serious attempt to solve it. Urban poverty in particular created home conditions that the Committee felt were 'the very opposite' of the child's 'natural biological environment' (Board of Education 1933, p. 119). The Report stated that:

> Bad housing, bad home environment, and economic hardship may be palliated and even ameliorated to nursery schools and classes; but the remedy calls for other action by the state and local authorities. The provision of schools, whatever be the scale on which is made, so long as these conditions survive, leaves untouched the problem of the child's early environment. (Board of Education 1933, p. 119)

The nursery school, therefore, was positioned by the Committee as 'a desirable adjunct to the national system of education' where local 'economic conditions' created an 'unsuitable environment' resulting in children under-five who:

> require careful attention to their physical welfare, and need to spend longer hours at school and to be provided with meals. (Board of Education 1933, pp. 187–88)

Although nursery provision could address the problems arising from the child's early environment, it and wider schooling in general could not, in the opinion of the Committee, solve and eradicate it; that would require a concerted, coordinated economic and social change.

6. Under-Fives in School in the 21st Century

In the period examined above, from 1861 to 1933, care and education provision for under-fives in England was hugely variable in scale and quality across England. In the absence of a focused state system of nursery provision, there was an expectation that private and voluntary institutions would make up much of the sector and that ideally families, and in particular mothers, would provide care and education in the home (Penn 2014). This largely continued to be the case until the end of the 20th century. However, in the late 1990s and early 2000s, the then New Labour government began to challenge aspects of this status quo. The period saw a vast increase in funding, the introduction of Children's Centers, but also a concomitant higher level of scrutiny for public and private early years provision. Increased early years provision was, to begin with, designed to offer universal services. However, the Sure Start policy was linked to an economic imperative focused on reducing 'welfare dependency' (Read 2015, p. 52). Getting parents, particularly lone parents the majority of whom were lone mothers, into the workplace and contributing to the economy required additional early years provision (Moss 2014; McDowall Clark and Baylis 2012). As well as the additional public provision, the New Labour government was committed to a continuation of a mixed public/private economy, covering private nurseries and childminders (as were the subsequent Coalition and Conservative governments), despite issues with the levels of poor quality in private childcare provision (Faulkner and Coates 2013). The non-statutory Curriculum Guidance for the Foundation Stage (CGFS) (Qualifications and Curriculum Authority QCA) was issued to schools with nursery and reception classes. This was followed by the publication of the non-statutory Birth to Three Matters guidance (Department for Education and Skills DfES) issued settings and individuals working with young children aged three and under. The Childcare Act 2006 (Great Britain 1918, c. 21) brought birth to five together, nominally removing the divide between care and education (McDowall Clark and Baylis 2012). By 2008 the Early Years Foundation Stage (EYFS) documentation was introduced with its statutory framework document (Department for Children, Schools and Families DCSF) and non-statutory practice guidance (Department for Children, Schools and Families DCSF). Within the space of a decade, the approach of primary schools to the education of under-fives had undergone significant changes.

6.1. The Report of the Independent Review on Poverty and Life Chances

With the 2008 global economic crash and, in the UK, the subsequent economic austerity of the Coalition government from 2010, funding for early years provision was drastically scaled back and increasingly targeted at a smaller sub-group of the poor (Lloyd 2015), who were heavily problematized in the policy discourse. On coming to power in 2010 the Coalition government of Conservatives and Liberal Democrats commissioned the 'Independent Review on Poverty and Life Chances', chaired by Labour Member of Parliament, Frank Field. It was charged by the then Prime Minister, David Cameron:

> to consider how home circumstances impact on children's life chances, and in particular how this home background determines a child's readiness for school. (Cabinet Office 2010, p. 12)

The final report, 'The Foundation Years: preventing poor children becoming poor adults', was published in December 2010 (Cabinet Office 2010). It set out an argument for funding of support for developing parenting skills and early education of children under five from economically disadvantaged backgrounds as the means of tackling child and cross-generational poverty and delivering social mobility. The introduction to the Report stated:

> It is family background, parental education, good parenting and the opportunities for learning and development in those crucial years that together matter more to children than money. (Cabinet Office 2010, p. 5)

The Report continued:

> while income is still important, it is not the exclusive or necessarily the dominant cause of poverty being handed on from one generation to another. The fact that non-income factors, such as the home learning environment and quality of childcare, are so important in deciding the fate of children has led us to construct a set of Life Chances Indicators. (Cabinet Office 2010, p. 12)

Thus, poverty was framed in the Report as a familial issue rather than a structural and economic issue. Therefore, against the backdrop of the Government's program of 'Austerity', which saw vast cuts at local and national level to a range of public services, the role of the state in relation to child poverty could be a narrow, education and care one, rather than an economic, employment, wages and benefits-driven one. The Report justified an individualized and localized focus on supporting the development of parental skills and funding for out-of-the-home education and care provision aimed at 'improving the abilities of our poorest children during the period when it is most effective to do so' (Cabinet Office 2010, p. 6). The Report argued:

> Children need nurturing far longer than any other species and the quality of this nurturing has a major impact on how well children develop and then fulfil their potential. This task is not primarily one that belongs to the state. We imperil the country's future if we forget that it is the aspirations and actions of parents which are critical to how well their children prosper. (Cabinet Office 2010, p. 11)

On the one hand, this statement argued that the role of nurturing, aspirational parent was not one that 'primarily ... belongs to the state', whilst it also framed the duty of individual parents as one that the government agencies needed to oversee for the good of the state. The emotive and pejorative phrase 'imperil the country's future' in particular framed parents in poverty as group that posed a national threat and therefore must be dealt with by the state. The Report continued by arguing for a raising of the status of what it called 'The Foundation Years', stating:

> The Foundation Years brings together all of the current services for children, from the womb until they go to school. The aim is that the Foundation Years will become, for the first time, an equal part of a new tripartite education system: the Foundation Years leading to the school years, leading in turn to further, higher and continuing education. (Cabinet Office 2010, p. 11)

Thus, by framing the Foundation Years as part of a tripartite 'education' system, the Report positioned the intervention of the state in the education of the youngest in society as beginning when the child was in utero. In an inversion of the 19th and 20th century worries about working class mothers being too keen to relinquish their parental duties to the state should early years provision be made to available for under-fives, a key concern of the Report (which was echoed in subsequent government publications on the roll-out of targeted early education provision for two-year-olds) was on the reluctance of families living in poverty to take up the provision. These discourses, underpinning this targeting of families living in poverty and in receipt of certain social security benefits, focused on them being 'hard to reach' and in some cases 'troubled'. The Report stated that respondents to the Review:

> believed that services must do much more to effectively engage parents who have traditionally been harder to reach. (Cabinet Office 2010, p. 88)

The Report was underpinned by Field's personal, somewhat rose-tinted and gendered view of parenting in the 1950s and his personal view that the 1960s had heralded a decline in the standard of parenting. In a section of the Report entitled 'Rupturing a good parenting tradition', Field argued:

> Geoffrey Gorer, the sociologist, noted in the early 1950s that the spread of a tough love style of parenting had been the agent that changed England from a centuries long tradition of brutality into what was remarked upon by visitors to these shores in the late nineteenth and early twentieth centuries as one of the most peaceful European nations. The tough love tradition of parenting did more than turn England into what was until recently a peaceful self governing kingdom ... But that tough love tradition has recently been in retreat. (Cabinet Office 2010, p. 18)

It must be noted that this valorization of standard of late 19th and early 20th century English working-class parenting stands in stark contrast to the highly critical views written during those times, as discussed earlier in this paper.

In contrast to the highly gendered assumptions of early years provision in the historic texts as aimed at and used by mothers, the Report also stated that a 'number of submissions also emphasized that children's services need to be more 'father-friendly'' (Cabinet Office 2010, p. 88). However, in Chapter 1 of the Report, entitled A Personal Commentary, Field's arguments tended to reinforce old-fashioned gender roles and to mourn their erosion since the economic changes of the late 20th century. The Report stated that 'de-industrialization destroyed more than the work ethic in many families and communities' (Cabinet Office 2010, p.18). The loss of their role as breadwinners working in male-dominated industry, the Report stated, meant that the 'major means by which many males were socialized into wider society was lost' (Cabinet Office 2010, p. 18). Similarly, the Report positioned the gendered, domestic and economically role of women in this industrialized 1950s society as one to which working class women themselves wished to return. It stressed the importance of full-time employment for fathers 'to family formation and stability' (Cabinet Office 2010, p. 25) but argued for part-time flexible employment for mothers, stating:

> The circumstances that made them most happy and contented are having a husband or partner in work so that they can combine their work and their family responsibilities in a pattern that gives primacy to their families. (Cabinet Office 2010, pp. 24–25)

The approach to poverty within the Field Report has tended to be repeated and reflected in policy and reports since 2010, and whatever their gender adults in poverty have been viewed in these discourses as inadequate to the role of parent and their children characterized as inherently and chronically vulnerable (Olusoga 2019). This has been underpinned by a 'catching up' discourse, that frames such children as inevitably 'falling behind' their better off peers academically (Gibb et al. 2010) due to 'gaps' caused by a lack of parental engagement in key tasks (Simpson 2013) such as reading stories that deny such children a state of 'school readiness'.

6.2. The Revised Early Years Foundation Stage Framework and 'School Readiness'

One of the recommendations from the Field Report was that funding needed to be provided to extend school-based early years provision to two-year-olds from such family backgrounds. From the initial brief of the Field Report, a discourse of 'school readiness' informed this expansion (Lloyd 2015) and was expressed in the revised EYFS framework (Department for Education DfE). In the introduction to the revised framework the second aim of the EYFS read:

> The Early Years Foundation Stage (EYFS) sets the standards that all early years providers must meet to ensure that children learn and develop well and are kept healthy and safe. It promotes teaching and learning to ensure children's 'school readiness' and gives children the broad range of knowledge and skills that provide the right foundation for good future progress through school and life. (Department for Education DfE, p. 2)

At the end of the EYFS, a key aim of the summative Foundation Stage profile was to report to 'parents and carers, practitioners and teachers' the child's 'readiness for Year 1' (Department for Education DfE, p. 11). Readiness for Year 1 was framed as being prepared for 'more formal learning' via a process in the reception year of a 'shift towards more activities led by adults' (Department for Education DfE, p. 6). This revised EYFS thus positioned under-fives as pupils in the making; children who must be made ready for the demands of the National Curriculum, particularly in relation to their becoming literate and numerate prior to the start of Year 1 (Moss 2014).

Alongside this school-readiness orientation, another key element of the revised EYFS has been the 'datafication' of the reception child (Robert-Holmes and Bradbury 2016) and the normative gaze of the Early Learning Goals (ELGs) and the expectation that children achieve a Good Level of Development (GLD). Ensuring school readiness has thus become positioned as the prime function of the EYFS. This is most especially felt in the reception year where the task of the teacher is increasingly focused on the reception child's ability to perform the role of the Year 1 child, and on an alignment of reception class practice with the alleged demands of the National Curriculum, Year 1 pedagogy and curriculum. However, further top-down pressure means that the pressure to conform to more formal practices in the reception year and to produce data, finds similar expression in work with younger children. Thus, paradoxically, the pressure to ensure school readiness becomes the driving force that restricts very young children's engagement with the play-based, child-initiated pedagogy. Whilst research suggests such play-based pedagogies best impact on their abilities for self-regulation, cognitive, physical and social development (Whitebread et al. 2012), the need for children under-five to be able to perform the role of 'pupil' in formal pedagogies for the over-fives impacts on the institutional spaces and practices in which they find themselves.

7. Discussion

Drawing together the strands of argument presented in this historical review of the subject of the care and education of children under five in schools allows some consideration of the changes and continuities in the official arguments presented. At each stage, discourses about social class and gender have informed debates on the nature and role of school-based provision, the needs of the child under five and the nature of parental responsibility.

7.1. The Nature and Role of School Provision for Under-Fives

In 1861, 1908 and 1933 discussion of school attendance for under-fives is torn between conflicting positions. One discourse positions the need for school-based provision for under-fives as unnatural, in that ideally the conditions that make it necessary should not exist. Another discourse positions it as necessary (but only for a sub-set of children) and if suitably designed, capable of compensating for a lack of 'natural' maternal nurturing. There is clear official preference for provision that is formal, school-based and under the scrutiny of inspection, rather than home-based or private provision. The materiality and space of schools as institutions for the under-five is a key focus of discussion. School spaces for under-fives must be adapted or built as spaces distinct from the home and the traditional spaces of elementary schooling. They must offer what is lacking in the home, namely safe and expansive indoor and outdoor spaces, play resources, interaction with adults who are a good influence, and scrutiny and measurement under the normative gaze of the school.

The impact of conflicting discourses is also evident in the 21st century. Whilst maternal employment is now largely seen as a positive, particularly as a means of lifting children out of poverty, the demands of parenting fall unevenly, and mothers tend still to be expected to shoulder the majority of the burden of work involved in the expected partnership between parents and school. Most children, of all social classes, now attend school at age four, in reception classes from the start of the academic year. The situation for younger children, however, is variable due to the fragmented nature of private and public nursery provision and the restricted nature of maternity and paternity pay. The failure of the New Labour government to develop and maintain universal services, the mixed economy of private and state provision and the partial nature of state funding for two, three and four-year-olds in nurseries all mean that in practice provision for under-fives is often divided along lines of social class. The EYFS espouses a discourse of play that requires provision of an enabling environment, space and resources to support indoor and outdoor activity and a holistic approach to learning. However, the focus on data, on development of early literacy and numeracy and on preparation for more formal learning in Year 1 pulls practice in the opposite direction.

7.2. Changing Conceptualizations of the Young Child

It is curiously hard to maintain a focus on the actual child in the historical discussion of school provision for under-fives. Where the child is discussed, the argument is often framed in relation to judgements made of the child's parents or about the institutions of home, care or education in which the child is contained. However, it is possible to discern how discourses of social class shape the reasoning about the child and the types of outcomes to be aimed at in schooling the child. The discussions in the 19th and 20th century texts examined all stress the difference between under-fives and older children and emphasize a need to develop provision that is distinctive and age-appropriate. In 1861 the working-class child is framed as a potential street-child and the focus and main purposes of nursery provision are to keep the child contained and to train the child in obedience. In 1908 the focus is on the child living in poverty, a child in physical and moral danger from home and from inadequate maternal care. Here provision must focus on the child's moral training, medical supervision, and organization into classes to facilitate transition into the elementary school. In 1933 the child is understood through the lens of psychology and through the now well-established measurement practices of school-based medical supervision. The child under five in nursery provision is not the norm; the natural place is in the home, with the mother, supported by access to medical supervision. For this subset of children, nursery provision conceptualizes the child as being comprised of physical, social and moral aspects that can be measured and impacted upon via the coordinated effort of professionals.

In the 21st century school is increasingly framed as the right place for the child under five. The EYFS has expanded school-based nursery provision, dismantled the practice of multiple intakes of rising fives in the reception year. The child under five is thus a school-child, a person to be cared for and educated simultaneously. Within the under-five label, however, there are now additional subsets. There is the reception year child, who is increasingly conceptualized as a latent Year 1 child, who can and should be treated as such in preparation for being one. The curriculum, and in particular the requirements of the next stage of the curriculum, becomes the scale against which the child is continually measured and judged. There is the two-year-old, from a disadvantaged background, who needs support to catch up. The two-year-old's attendance at school positions education as an intervention capable of offsetting the effects of structural poverty.

7.3. Changing Conceptualizations of Parental Responsibility

Changing conceptualizations of parental responsibility can be detected across the historic documents discussed above, particularly in the language used to target and describe and problematize parenting in poverty and the role of the mother. However, two threads of continuity can be found in this shifting discourse. Firstly, working-class parents in poverty are talked about and not to. The perspectives presented in reports are those of professionals working in education and related fields and the officials on boards and committees. Working-class parents living in poverty are considered responsible for and productive of their marginalized social and economic status. Furthermore, the right of the state to develop state apparatus to intervene in their parenting decisions is framed as a social and moral duty for the social, physical and economic health of the nation (Hendrick 1997).

Secondly, these changing conceptualizations of parental responsibility are informed by discourses of gender. In 1861 and 1908 heavy emphasis is placed on the mother. Her place is inside the home and her purpose is to do her maternal duty. The stay at home mother in a good home is an ideal, based on middle class values and privileged economic circumstances. Maternal employment is couched primarily as female selfishness and poverty and poor surroundings as the moral failings of profligacy and lack of effort. The need to compensate for the negative impact of such mothers and homes is countered, however, by a concern that nursery provision may undermine parental responsibility and reward laziness. School provision therefore is to be limited and targeted at a class of family with the understanding that the discipline of school attendance falls as much on the parent as on the child. In the 1933 Report, there is less emphasis on the pejorative discussion of women's employment, maybe reflecting the desperate economic conditions of the economic depression at the time. Instead, nursery school is framed as actively promoting greater parental responsibility, and enhanced by the establishment of classes for mothers, open days for parents and the involvement of parents in supporting the material resourcing of the provision. Although fathers are mentioned and expected to show an interest in their child's schooling, childcare is still framed as the duty of mothers and something for which school needs to prepare girls and not boys.

In the early 21st century, reflecting changes in social norms and family composition, there is a focus in policy on lone parents and parents on social security benefits. Rather than being based on judgements about 'bad housing', it is dependency on welfare benefits that is foregrounded as problematic and potentially productive of a passing on of the 'habit' of poverty between generations. Expanded early years provision is positioned as enabling parents (especially lone mothers) to gain employment, contribute to the economy and in so doing, avoid passing on to their children the 'habit' of being in poverty. In the Field Report, however, we see a discourse that whilst promoting 'father-friendly' practice, also positions men as ideally the main breadwinners, working full time and mothers as the main care-givers whose employment should ideally be part-time and flexible. Though the reasoning has shifted, throughout the period, early years provision has been framed as a potential remedy for the social and economic failings of the poor; failings that are often characterized as moral in character. Over recent years a specific social group has been targeted and state provision has been designed to remove the children of that group from the home at an earlier age and for longer periods of time. This state provision has maintained a focus on dividing, sorting and treating children under-five, informed by practices of measurement and the gathering of data. Over time the nature of the data harvested from children has shifted. The early 20th century focus was medically-informed, centred on physical health and development. In the early 21st century this has become a curriculum and accountability-driven focus on school-readiness, as manifested in children's ability to demonstrate their developing literacy and numeracy (Robert-Holmes and Bradbury 2016). Parental responsibility is now tied to discourses of emergent literacy that emphasize the role of speech, story-telling and social interaction and that frame parents in poverty as inevitably creating gaps in their children's experience that must be filled by the state.

Funding: This research received no external funding.

Conflicts of Interest: The author declares no conflict of interest.

References

Aldrich, Richard. 2006. *Lessons from History of Education: The Selected Works of Richard Aldrich*. Abingdon: Routledge.
Board of Education. 1905a. *Code of Regulations for Public Elementary Schools with Schedules*. London: HMSO.
Board of Education. 1905b. *Reports on Children under Five Years of Age in Public Elementary Schools by Women Inspectors of the Board of Education*. London: HMSO.
Board of Education. 1908. *Report of the Consultative Committee upon the School Attendance of Children Below the Age of Five*. London: HMSO.
Board of Education. 1933. *Report of the Consultative Committee on Infant and Nursery Schools*. London: HMSO.
Cabinet Office. 2010. *The Foundation Years: Preventing Poor Children Becoming Poor Adults. The Report of the Independent Review on Poverty and Life Chances*. London: Crown Copyright.
Cremaschi, Sergio. 2014. *Utilitarianism and Malthus' Virtue Ethics*. London: Routledge.
Department for Children, Schools and Families (DCSF). 2008a. *Practice Guidance for the Early Years Foundation Stage*. London: DSCF.
Department for Children, Schools and Families (DCSF). 2008b. *Statutory Framework for the Early Years Foundation Stage*. London: DCSF.
Department for Education (DfE). 2012. *Statutory Framework for the Early Years Foundation Stage: Setting the Standards for Learning, Development and Care for Children from Birth to Five*. London: Crown Copyright.
Department for Education and Skills (DfES). 2002. *Birth to Three Matters*. London: DfES.
Education Commission. 1861a. *The Newcastle Report. Report of the Commissioners Appointed to Inquire into the State of Popular Education in England*. London: HMSO.
Education Commission. 1861b. *The Newcastle Report Volume VI. Minutes of Evidence Taken Before the Commissioners*. London: HMSO.
Foucault, Michel. 1970. *The Order of Things*. London: Tavistock.
Foucault, Michel. 1972. *The Archaeology of Knowledge*. London: Tavistock.
Foucault, Michel. 1977. *Discipline and Punish: The Birth of the Prison*. London: Allen Lane.
Faulkner, Dorothy, and Elizabeth A. Coates. 2013. Early childhood policy and practice in England: Twenty years of change. *International Journal of Early Years Education* 21: 244–63. [CrossRef]
Gibb, Jennifer, Helena Jelicic, Ivana La Valle, Sally Gowland, Rachel Kinsella, Patricia Jessiman, and Rachel Ormston. 2010. Rolling out Free Early Education for Disadvantaged Two Year Olds: An Implementation Study for Local Authorities and Providers. Available online: https://assets.publishing.service.gov.uk/government/uploads/system/uploads/attachment_data/file/181502/DFE-RR131.pdf (accessed on 13 April 2019).
Great Britain. 1918. *Education Act 8 & 9, Geo. 5. C. 39*. London: HMSO.
Great Britain. 2006. *Childcare Act c. 21*. London: HMSO.

House of Commons Debate. 1870. Elementary Education (re-committed) Bill—[BILL 167]. *Hansard* vol. 203: 41–95.

Heathorn, Stephen. 2000. *For Home, Country and Race: Constructing Gender, Class, and Englishness in the Elementary School, 1880–1914*. Toronto: University of Toronto Press Inc.

Hendrick, Harry. 1997. *Children, Childhood and English Society, 1880–1990*. Cambridge: Cambridge University Press.

Lloyd, Eva. 2015. Early Childhood Education and Care Policy in England under the Coalition Government. *London Review of Education* 13: 144–56. [CrossRef]

McDowall Clark, Rory, and Sue Baylis. 2012. "Wasted down there": Policy and practice with the under-threes. *Early Years* 32: 229–42. [CrossRef]

Moss, Peter. 2014. Early childhood policy in England 1997–2013: Anatomy of a missed opportunity. *International Journal of Early Years Education* 22: 346–58. [CrossRef]

Office for Standards in Education (Ofsted). 2017. Bold Beginnings: The Reception Curriculum in a Sample of Good and Outstanding Primary Schools. Manchester. Available online: https://www.gov.uk/government/publications/reception-curriculum-in-good-and-outstanding-primary-schools-bold-beginnings (accessed on 3 January 2018).

Olusoga, Yinka. 2019. The Contemporary Environment. In *Supporting Vulnerable Children in the Early Years*. Edited by Pat Beckley. London: Jessica Kingsley Publishers.

Palmer, Amy. 2011. Nursery schools for the few or the many? Childhood, education and the State in mid-twentieth-century England. *Paedagogica Historica* 47: 139–54. [CrossRef] [PubMed]

Penn, Helen. 2014. *Understanding Early Childhood: Issues and Controversies*, 3rd ed. Maidenhead: Open University Press.

Qualifications and Curriculum Authority (QCA). 2000. *Curriculum Guidance for the Foundation Stage*. London: Department for Education and Employment.

Read, Jane. 2015. Transformation and regulation: A century of continuity in nursery school and welfare policy rhetoric. *Journal of Education Policy* 30: 39–61. [CrossRef]

Reisigl, Martin, and Ruth Wodak. 2016. The Discourse-Historical Approach (DHA). In *Methods of Critical Discourse Studies*, 3rd ed. Edited by Ruth Wodak and Michael Meyer. London: Sage, pp. 23–61.

Robert-Holmes, Guy, and Alice Bradbury. 2016. Governance, accountability and the datafication of early years education in England. *British Educational Research Journal* 42: 600–61. [CrossRef]

Simpson, Donald. 2013. Remediating Child Poverty Via Preschool: Exploring Practitioners' Perspectives in England. *International Journal of Early Years Education* 21: 85–96. [CrossRef]

Whitebread, David, Marisol Basilio, Martina Kuvalja, and Mohini Verma. 2012. The Importance of Play: A Report on the Value of Children's Play with a Series of Policy Recommendations. Available online: http://www.importanceofplay.eu/IMG/pdf/dr_david_whitebread_-_the_importance_of_play.pdf (accessed on 26 March 2018).

© 2019 by the author. Licensee MDPI, Basel, Switzerland. This article is an open access article distributed under the terms and conditions of the Creative Commons Attribution (CC BY) license (http://creativecommons.org/licenses/by/4.0/).

Article

Margaret McMillan's Contributions to Cultures of Childhood

Betty Liebovich

Educational Studies Department, Goldsmiths University of London, London SE14 6NW, UK; b.liebovich@gold.ac.uk

Received: 30 April 2019; Accepted: 19 July 2019; Published: 25 July 2019

Abstract: Margaret McMillan is widely known for her open-air nursery, making it her life mission to live by the McMillan family motto, *Miseris Succurrere Disco*, which translates to 'I endeavour to care for the less fortunate'. Margaret and her sister, Rachel, dedicated their lives to improving living conditions for the poor and working class in England and created health and dental clinics for them in Bradford, Bow and Deptford. During the 1889 Dock Strike, Margaret and Rachel supported workers by marching and demonstrating at Parliament. At the turn of the last century, they were instrumental in inspiring legislation for children's welfare and education on both local and national levels in England. Their efforts led to campaigning for the 1906 Provision of School Meals Act and medical inspections for primary school children. In an effort to improve health conditions for the children living in the Deptford community, they created night camps for deprived children in 1908. With war impending in 1914, they created the first open air nursery in England in order to serve the disadvantaged community surrounding it, providing a safe and nurturing learning environment for the young children of the women going to work in place of the men who were called up to war. Margaret McMillan's ideals for young children's nurture and education continue to influence how we educate children in contemporary England and are woven into the fabric of our goals for young children's futures.

Keywords: early-years education history; open-air nursery; early-years education

1. Introduction

Christian Socialists in the 19th century organised in response to the political, economic, social and religious developments in the mid-Victorian period with the intent of reducing inequalities within society in general. At the heart of Christian Socialism was a commitment to collectivism and cross-class cooperation, avoiding proposals or policies (Williams 2016), rather than engaging in the competition driven by an industrialist society. As Christian Socialists, Rachel and Margaret McMillan focused their efforts on improving the lives of the poor and working class of England, concentrating their attention on young children to prepare them for a better future. By establishing health and dental clinics for people living in deprivation in Bradford, Bow and Deptford, campaigning for the 1906 Provision of School Meals Act and creating night camps for deprived children in Deptford in 1908, they took steps to improve the life chances of children who might otherwise find themselves caught in a cycle of poverty.

"At the end of the 19th century, childhood acquired a new significance. Children—especially working-class children—became symbols of social hope, of a better and healthier future, of individuality and selfhood" (Steedman 1990, foreword). The demands of industrialization meant that children became a resource—cheap labour in factories and mines to perform simple tasks at a lower wage than an adult would earn (Griffin 2014). However, the Boer War led to the discovery that through medical inspections, "one third of volunteers was unfit for military service. It appeared that the physical condition of the working class male prevented him from fighting, as well as working effectively in his job" (BBC 2019). A new perspective of children and their health and welfare became a societal focus with the establishment of The National Society for the Prevention of Cruelty to Children (NSPCC), which was founded in 1889, and earlier, in 1870, the Education Act became the foundation for compulsory education for all children. A shift from viewing children as little adults led to them going to school instead of working. Children became a national resource that required a healthy upbringing so that they might be fit for work and military service.

In March of 1914, the threat of World War I (WWI) was impending, and the McMillan sisters launched the opening of their open-air nursery for the youngest children living in the tenements of Deptford. At the turn of the last century, this area of London experienced extreme deprivation with a shortage of space, clean and affordable housing and few well-paid jobs (Bradburn, issues children and 1976). Families were living in an overcrowded and congested community with a lack of infrastructure to support the dense population, leading to children experiencing a host of untreated health issues and social deficits, which the McMillan sisters were determined to address so that these children could have the childhood they deserved. The nursery was designed to provide these children with a chance to experience clean clothing and healthy food and have space to learn in fresh air, allowing them a start in life that could change the trajectory of their future.

2. Biographical Information

Margaret and Rachel spent their childhood in upstate New York, taking advantage of the plethora of outdoor space surrounding their home. Margaret describes their childhood:

> It is a very happy life. Our parents are modern and American in their ideas of how we shall be brought up. They impose no needless restrictions on us, and do not overwhelm us with the Atlas of unreasoning and almighty authority- and yet we are not left to the mercy of impulse and riot of selfish instinct. (McMillan 1927, p. 10)

This idyllic start to life was the impetus for the McMillan sisters to offer a similar start to children living in deprivation in South East London. Unlike many children of their era, the McMillan sisters had the freedom of play and movement outdoors. Children in England were expected to work the land or labour in factories, often living in harsh conditions in large cities. Their childhood in America shaped who these women became and what they believed they could offer young children living in deprivation. Their young lives changed dramatically, leading to their convictions in adulthood about the experiences a young child needed.

Tragedy befell the McMillan family when their father and younger sister, Elizabeth, passed away from illness. Margaret also had the illness that took the lives of their sister and father, and although she survived, she suffered from significant hearing loss that was not restored until she was around 14 years of age. The loss was devastating for their mother who took the girls back to Scotland to live with the McMillan family. Their mother felt she needed family support to raise the girls and offer them a better life than she could provide on her own. Margaret wrote: "So, in September [1865], we three went on board the good ship City of Boston, for Liverpool, en route for Inverness" (McMillan 1927, p. 12).

Despite these setbacks, Rachel and Margaret received a good education in Scotland. Margaret, however, found living with her family in Scotland to be restrictive and resented the strictness imposed on her. Gratefully leaving Scotland when she was 18 years old, she studied humanities subjects in Germany before becoming a governess for various wealthy families there. These experiences offered Margaret an opportunity to understand the resources afforded to children of affluent families, and she began formulating her ideas for changing the lives of working-class children. Additionally, having been introduced to people of influence, she learned to use her oratory and personal skills to gain the resources she needed from these influential people to create social change in her endeavours to improve the lives of working-class families.

Toward the end of the 1800s, Margaret needed a change from working for the wealthy elite in Germany and moved to London. At the same time, Rachel, in Scotland caring for her ailing grandmother, discovered Christian Socialism, educating herself through publications by William Morris (a socialist activist associated with the British Arts and Crafts Movement) and William Thomas Stead (a pioneer of investigative journalism), and after July 1888, she joined her sister in London. Here, she converted Margaret to Christian Socialism, and together, they attended political meetings, where they met influential socialist activists William Morris, H. M. Hyndman (who launched Britain's first left-wing political party), Peter Kropotkin (a proponent of a decentralised communist society free from central government),William Stead (noted for reportage on child welfare, social legislation and reformation of England's criminal codes) and Ben Tillett (British socialist, trade union leader and politician). The McMillan sister's involvement in the Christian Socialist movement challenged the child labour of working-class children, their exploitation and the abuse they experienced. Factory owners in the Victorian Era put profit before safety, and children were expected to work twelve-hour days—the same as adults. Children often worked in dangerous conditions, leading to injury if not death, and were not paid well because of their age. Although there was legislation attempting to address the exploitation of children in the work force (1833 Factory Act, Mines and Collieries Act 1842, 1844 Factory Act and the Factory Act of 1847 (Ten Hours Act)), children continued to be employed to work long hours in poor conditions (Griffin 2014). In an attempt to actively engage with their Christian Socialist views of addressing social inequalities, Rachel and Margaret engaged in the 1889 London Dock Strike, marching and protesting at Parliament. Margaret's activities for social change led to membership in the Fabian Society, the Labour Church, the Social Democratic Federation and the Independent Labour Party (ILP) (Steedman 1990). Rachel was incensed about the working class and "their stinted opportunities, their poor pay roused in her a storm of feeling that could not but find some outlet in action" (McMillan 1917, p. 170). Margaret continued her efforts to create change by teaching young women in the East End, publicly speaking out about the need for addressing social inequalities and using investigative journalism (inspired by William Thomas Stead) to publish her ideals of creating social change (Steedman 1990).

Margaret secured a position on the Bradford School Board as a representative in November 1894, quickly becoming renowned as an active social reformer with a specific interest in child welfare. She was re-elected to the school board in 1900, but the 1902 Education Bill soon became law, eradicating school boards and giving control and management of primary schools to the district and county councils. Women were no longer eligible to be elected to these councils, and Margaret lost her position and power to create social change. Although disappointed, Margaret joined Rachel, a health and hygiene teacher, in Bromley, London.

"It was she [Rachel] who gave me [Margaret] the first impulse to social work, and pointed out to me the wrongs of the disinherited, the landless, the child-labourer" (McMillan 1917, p. 170). In the interest of addressing children's health, in 1906, Margaret and Rachel canvassed for compulsory medical inspections of school children (McMillan 1927, p. 118), which was subsequently realised in the Education (Administrative Procedures) Bill of 1907. This bill led to the establishment of a children's health nurse in all primary schools to track children's health while in school. Noting the poverty and subsequent health issues in Deptford, they established community health and dental clinics in this suitably 'needy' area of London in which Margaret had been a manager of primary schools and had become familiar with the community and the challenges they faced. In her attempt to break the cycle of poverty, she envisioned offering children a healthy lifestyle. The McMillan sisters used their connections to secure housing on Evelyn Street in Deptford, first to establish health clinics for the working poor in the immediate community and then to create night camps for girls from ages 6–14 in 1908, where they were provided with a hot evening meal, bathing facilities and clothes washing and a cot to sleep outdoors. This afforded them the advantage of fresh air and nutritious food they would not receive in their family abode. With the huge success of this initiative, they expanded this service to local boys as well, encouraging them to leave the crowded and unhealthy tenements in which they lived every evening for a healthier alternative, making sure everyone had hot nutritious food, clean clothing and bedding.

3. Context

Deptford in 1899 was a bleak and dismal area in South East London where labourers flocked in the hopes of gaining stable employment in the bordering dockyards or the Woolwich arsenal. Unfortunately, there were more workers than jobs, leading to cramped, congested streets, inadequate housing and rampant poverty. Rather than acquiring gainful employment, these hopeful individuals became "occasional labourers, loafers and semi-criminals" (Fried and Elman 1969, p. 9). In 1899, Booth wrote "There is struggling poverty, there is destitution, there is hunger, drunkenness, brutality and crime" (Fried and Elman 1969, p. 4).

At the beginning of the 20th century, the streets where the nursery was located were described as follows:

> From the corner of High St. a new road has been cut through to Creek Rd, continuous with Evelyn Street, the road on which the nursery is located and where the McMillan sisters lived), involving demolition of a great part of Wellington St. and Queen St. It is named Creek Road. Land is cleared and the LCC (London County Council) advertise it 'to let' except a plot near east end where a new Deptford Fund House is being erected. (Steele 1996, p. 137)

This land that the LCC offered 'to let' was locally referred to as "the Stowage", which the McMillan sisters rented to establish their nursery.

According to Steele (1996), "Of all the pre-occupations of the late-Victorian period, prostitution rank[ed] highly" (p. 12), and Deptford was no exception. In his notebooks documenting the neighbourhoods of London, Booth described Deptford as inhabited by "casters [market hawkers], prostitutes and nightly fights" (Steele 1996, p. 11). Booth's general remarks about Deptford in 1899 stated that "Most of the people living here work at one of the factories along the Creek. Beside the Chemical works, there are numerous business places employing a large number of 'hands' (Steele 1996, p. 139). When Margaret and Rachel moved to Deptford, they encountered similar, if not worse, conditions, as Booth observed. In descriptions of walks taken, Booth evokes images of the people he encountered in the street: " ... some casters and prostitutes, shoeless children running about and frowsy women gaping at the doors" (Steele 1996, p. 137). It was these shoeless children that the McMillan sisters encountered when they moved to Deptford and for whom they opened the clinic on Evelyn Street in the early 1900s. The sisters had grave concerns for these children, noting that they were playing in crowded and congested streets and living in crowded and insanitary conditions with nowhere safe to play and spend their time. What they envisioned for them was a similar setting in which they were raised in the United States—fresh air, healthy food and plenty of space and time for freely chosen outdoor play.

Margaret's work as a school board visitor was, according to Booth (Fried and Elman 1969, p. 3) to "perform amongst them a house-to-house visitation; every house in every street is in their books, and details are given of every family with children of school age". It was through this work that Margaret gained insight into the plight of the young children living in tenement housing in Deptford and the dire need to support them in order to break the cycle of poverty. This was also how she was made aware of the property that was being let by the LCC when she and Rachel were considering opening the nursery. Booth stated that "The children are the street arabs [sic], and are to be found separated from the parents m pauper or industrial schools" (Fried and Elman 1969, p. 12), offering a succinct and miserable outlook on childhood and children's futures in this area of South East London. The McMillan sisters set out to change this.

As noted above, the piece of land that the McMillan sisters rented for their nursery was referred to by the locals as 'the Stowage', and this label continues to be used in contemporary times. Up until the mid-1800s, there were working docks along the Thames, a short walk from the Stowage, and according to local history, illegally acquired goods from the docks were stored on this property. Simultaneously, in anticipation of the impending war (WWI), funding to maintain the nursery was aided by a national drive for childcare that would allow women to undertake work outside the home as part of the war effort, and the sisters approached the Ministry of Munitions via the Board of Education, offering to care for the children of women working in munitions factories. For this service, the nursery received a grant of 7d (3p)[1] a day for each child of a munition worker. The nursery opened its doors in late March of 1914, and "the children who first entered the camp-87 in all-the eldest was five, and the youngest three months old" came from the surrounding community in Deptford (McMillan 1917, p. 51). The nursery was the step forward that the McMillan sisters envisioned to improve the lives of the young children whom they deemed worthy of enjoying a healthy childhood with access to fresh air, a nourishing diet and supportive adults in an educational environment encouraging child-directed, outdoor play.

She described her refreshed mission as "millions of children needing nurture, millions of women doing work for which they had no real preparation and no real help" (McMillan 1927, p. 96). With their Christian Socialist ethos, the McMillan sisters made the conscious decision to improve the lives of the working poor, particularly the children living in the tenement slums around the docks and throughout Deptford by offering young children a healthier start in life.

4. The McMillans' Views of Childhood

Victorian English society had specific ideals for young children, and their definition of childhood was limited and limiting. Historical accounts of Victorian childhood include "little children who should be seen and not heard, under-tens slaving away in cotton factories and coal mines" (Cunningham 2006, p. 140). "In the late nineteenth century, and in the years up to the First World War, childhood was reconceptualised in British society-that is to say, children became the subjects of legislative attention and formed the basis of various accounts of social development as they had not done before" (Steedman 1990, p. 62). In the century before Margaret began working to improve the childhoods of the working-class, intense concentration had been focused on working-class children at different points, including them in government policy. Building on the campaigning for the 1906 Provision of School Meals Act, Margaret noted that the children whose lives they hoped to improve were victims of a system in which "Poverty of experience or impressions-whether from the closure of any gate of sense, or through any other cause—induce[d] a permanent and irremediable weakness in the mental life" (McMillan 1900, p. 8) of the young child. The population of children living in such deprivation was experiencing the outcomes of the "unprecedented speed of the economic and social changes in Britain consequent to the Industrial Revolution of the late eighteenth century and early nineteenth ... The cities and towns grew at an exponential rate, creating enormous social problems, not least for the children" (Cunningham 2006, p. 140). These children had little joy in their stunted childhood and were expected to enter the labour force at very early ages.

In the early 1900s, Ruskin described a walk he took in the area, looking at the children playing in the streets "and consider[ing] 'the marvel [of] ... how the race resists, at least in its childhood, influences of ill-regulated birth, poisoned food, poisoned air and soul neglect'" (Ruskin 1906, p. 390). In Deptford as a whole, the infant mortality rates in 1909 and 1910 were 104 and 124 per thousand. However, in the east ward (Margaret's main catchment area) in the same years, they were 136 and 189 per thousand; that is, roughly one-fifth of the children born in this ward did not survive their first year of life McMillan 1927, p. 37).

In order to combat such a waste of human potential, Margaret drew on her own experiences of a rural childhood without want and with woods in which to run and play. This gave her a clear vision of what she wanted for the children of Deptford:

> She [Margaret] realized that poverty, ignorance and disease were not only harming an adult population, but mortgaging the growth of the next generation also. She yearned to change the system which created the conditions she abhorred. At the same time she realized that sick children could not wait for political reform. She fought to cure the dirt and disease that

---

[1] 7d was 7 pence which translates into 3 pence in contemporary money.

she saw every day in the mothers and children round her, and the fight for political reform as well. (Bradburn 1976, pp. 45–46)

Rejecting the Victorian view that children need to conform to quiet complacency, Margaret reflected Froebelian ideals, asserting that "the first years are years of opportunity. If during those years good fundamental impressions are made, muscle and nerve is trained, dormant faculties roused, right habits formed, and the whole nervous system rendered capable of full exercise, and fine nutrition, then the power to do well is acquired" (McMillan 1900, p. 35). In the era in which the McMillan sisters hoped to create change for these young children's lives, they attempted to remedy a historical childhood of child labour, child exploitation and child abuse. Margaret and Rachel envisioned ideal early years for young children, characterized by experiences involving unlimited outdoor play, child-facilitated learning and nutritious food. Children would have access to medical attention as needed, and their health would be monitored regularly to ensure that they were growing and developing without the complications of unhealthy living in cramped housing with limited access to resources. The children in Deptford were plagued by recurring illnesses and lacked access to medical resources, sufficient food (particularly healthy food) and large, safe spaces to play, learn and develop.

5. The Nursery

Margaret and Rachel McMillan began their work in Deptford during the "revisionist Froebelian child-saving ideology" (Brehony, p. 185), inspired by their Christian Socialist affiliations rather than their familiarity with or convictions about Froebelian pedagogy. The following two Froebelian principles were reflected in Margaret and Rachel's views of what the children living in poverty in Deptford deserved:

1. Childhood is seen as valid in itself, as part of life and not simply as preparation for adulthood. Thus education is seen similarly as something of the present and not just preparation and training for later.
2. The whole child is considered to be important. Health–physical and mental is emphasised, as well as the importance of feelings and thinking and spiritual aspects (Bruce 1987, p. 16).

They ruminated that "it is the open space that matters. Our rickety children, our cramped, and even (in many cases) deformed children, get back to the ear with its magnetic currents, and the free blowing wind" (McMillan 1917, p. 52). They envisioned opportunities for these urban children living in squalor and congestion: "To let them [children] live at last and have the sight of people planting and digging, to let them run and work and experiment, sleep, have regular meals, the sights and sounds of winter and spring, autumn and summer" (McMillan 1917, p. 52). Knowing that the young children living in poverty required their whole being to be considered, they envisioned that "Space, and more space, is what toddlers want. To move, to use their new power of getting about, is for them a tremendous experience" (McMillan 1917, p. 58). Their vision of offering a better childhood experience for these young children was spurred by their encounters with the children enrolling in the nursery:

> Some children come to us crippled already by restraint. In some cases there is deformity even in the first and second years. The legs are bandy, or one leg drawn up; the wrists feeble through want of exercise; the head pushed forward, the mouth wide and hanging open. (McMillan 1917, p. 61)

Knowing that they could provide a better start in life for the deprived children in Deptford, the McMillan sisters were not daunted by seeing "Many [children] arrive at the nursery utterly stupefied by neglect" (McMillan 1917, p. 160).

With war impending, the McMillan sisters were able to gain funding from the government to provide nursery care for young children. World War I—with men being conscripted into the armed forces and the overwhelming number of casualties—created the need for married women with young children to be recruited to work in the ammunition factories in neighbouring Woolwich (the location of the Royal Artillery since the 17th century, employing 80,000 workers during WWI). The needs of the war also led to these mothers being employed by rail services, driving public transport vehicles, nursing, working as mechanics for the Women's Royal Air and on farms in the Women's Land Army.

While these mothers worked, their children were offered a safe, nurturing learning environment that catered to the whole child, not just their minds. The expansive garden had trees for climbing, vegetable and flower gardens for tending, climbing structures for physical development and cots for children to have their afternoon nap in the fresh air.

Margaret felt strongly that teachers were the heart of young children's learning and development. "Teachers are the captains and the ammunition of the teaching world . . . . we need . . . teacher-nurses, not mere 'minders' of children" (McMillan 1917, p. 159). Nursery education during the time that the McMillan sisters created their nursery was typically privately funded and fee-paying. The teachers in nurseries were often well intended women who had little background in children's learning and development. Margaret McMillan wrote:

> In 1919 there were very few Nursery Schools of any kind, and no large open-air Nursery School that I know of other than our own. As for the training of teachers it was not even considered as yet, so confused, so blind indeed was the general view on this. Many people believed that training of any kind was unnecessary for a nursery teacher, just as they still believe that it is quite unnecessary for the woman who is a mother. Nursery Schools were to be a dumping-ground for the well intentioned but dull women of that day. (McMillan 1930, p. 4)

The McMillan sisters deliberately created a learning environment, situated in the community in which the children lived, that allowed them to explore learning in the outdoors with a play space overlooking the local community—the children's community. The nursery was designed to tackle the children's ongoing physical and mental health through daily baths, clean clothing, fresh air, play and three meals each day. Although the nursery drew on Froebel's influences and pedagogical approaches, the McMillans' ethos for teaching young children was less philosophical, and the focus went beyond cognitive education. "The nursery" (as it was known at that time) began with the ideals of supporting children's learning, as well as addressing the needs and development of the whole child. Similar to Froebel, their philosophy was that children learn by exploring and that they would achieve their full potential through first-hand experience and active learning. Unlike Froebel, there were no "gifts" or specific educative materials used to develop the children's understanding, although Margaret had very specific ideas of what resources the children required and what they needed to gain from their experiences. The sisters stressed the importance of free play, regularly through craft and water activities, with most learning transpiring in the outdoors—providing large and varied external areas for these investigations.

The nursery was organised to take advantage of the green space bordered by enclosed areas called shelters, where the children could go if they wanted to have a quieter area for learning. The community in which they lived was congested and overcrowded, and the garden space in which the children spent the majority of their learning time offered them a well-developed garden for exploring, playing and developing in the fresh air that was not afforded outside their learning environment (Bradburn 1976). Additionally, there was a roof-top play space to enable the children to view their surrounding community in contrast to the lush and nurturing learning environment. Included in the outdoor area were trees, a vegetable garden (which provided some of the food used in lunch and dinners), flowers, trees, pets, chickens to provide eggs for meals, climbing structures, a stage for plays and oration, trikes/bikes/scooters and a multitude of other materials for the children to explore and learn. The shelters bordering the garden provided indoor space for the children to play and learn, should they choose. The shelters offered more quiet space and protection from the extreme elements.

The nursery opened at 07:30, so that mothers could drop their children off on the way to their factory work. Most arrived between 08:00 and 09:00. Upon arrival, the children were each given a bath and changed into nursery school clothing, which was washed every evening to be fresh for the next day. Every child was given a breakfast of very nourishing porridge and milk, sometimes accompanied by a piece of crusty bread, which was intended to help them strengthen their teeth through chewing. After breakfast, at 09:00, 'lessons' began. Morning hours saw the children engaged in their learning either in the garden or in the shelters, depending on the weather. Lunch was served between 11:30 and 12:00, with children over 3 years of age serving themselves from dishes passed around by a server (another child). Following lunch, the older children were responsible for clearing the tables and setting out the camp beds and blankets in the garden for the midday rest. After the midday rest, children engaged in free play, music and games, all overseen by teachers mentored by Margaret and Rachel. Before the children left for the day, they had a meal served at 16:00 to ensure that they all had the proper nourishment required for their development. Most children were collected by their mothers after their work, typically between 17:00 and 17:30 (Steedman 1990).

Margaret and Rachel planned the nursery day to promote all aspects of young children's development in addition to fostering good health, happiness and respect for others. Reflecting their ideals of Christian Socialists, "these were the characteristics, handed down from the philosophies of the enlightenment, that were deemed essential in ensuring children's wellbeing in adulthood and the production of a just and caring society" (Giardiello 2014, p. 63).

Margaret was passionate about the importance of well 'trained' teachers, as she felt that children were being 'cheated' by being subjected to inadequately educated teachers. In her opinion, the proposed teaching programme of two years with two teaching practices was insufficient, and she believed that the job of educating young children could not be achieved without more rigorous and more extensive training. Margaret repeatedly encountered trained teachers who could not cope with the poverty of the community, falling into despair when confronted with large classes of deprived children According to Margaret, the importance of the teacher's interactions with the child is not just the spoken language, because "the tone of the teacher is more to him [the child] than her [the teacher's] words" (McMillan 1900, p. 11).

Margaret's ethos for young children's learning was based on the firm belief that teachers of young children required a three-year teacher education programme in order to be fully prepared for the challenges of the job. "Margaret's experience with the teachers she encountered made her realise the urgent need for specific training for those who intended to work with the disadvantaged pre-school children. Consequently she decided to initiate courses for teachers and to use the Nursery School as an integral part of their training" (Bradburn 1976, p. 183). Many teachers in the nursery were educated to embrace the principles and practices of Froebel—the apostle of play. "Formal teaching is a very trivial matter in comparison with the vital education given through impressions" (McMillan 1900, p. 11). Eventually, in 1930, a year prior to her death, Margaret realised her dream of opening a teacher training school adjacent to the property on which the nursery was situated, and on 6 May 1930, Queen Mary formally opened the Rachel McMillan Training College.

6. Impact on the Provision of Early-Years Education

Provisions for young children's learning in England have continued to reflect the McMillan sister's ethos for young children living in deprivation and the McMillan family motto, *Miseris Succurrere Disco* (I learn to care for the unfortunate). Play is still at the heart of young children's education in the early-years foundation stage in that a reference learning environment and outdoor play are highly encouraged, reflecting the open-air ethos in the McMillan nursery. A focus on partnerships with families continues to be prioritised, providing continuity for young children (Early Years Foundation Stage).

The Hadow Report (1933) used the McMillan nursery as a benchmark for exemplary education for young children. In the introduction, the report states that "we have made particular reference to the teaching and practical achievement of that great exemplar of nursery education in England, Margaret McMillan" (p. xix).

An outline of experiences for young children's nursery education reflected the McMillans' ethos and the influence of Froebel's ideals for developmentally appropriate learning, stating that:

> The daily programme of the school comprises a succession of happy and joyous pursuits and activities in which the distinction between work and play disappears. The children work when they think they are playing, and play when they think they are working. The educational influences in nursery schools derive largely from Froebel, Madame Montessori and Margaret McMillan. (Hadow Report 1933, p. 104)

The Hadow Report (1933) also exemplified the need for young children to learn outdoors, asserting that "It is clearly essential that the nursery school should be placed within easy distance of the homes which it is intended to serve, and this consideration in practice imposes a limit on the possible size of the school" (p. 107). When extolling the virtues of outdoor learning, the report goes on to say:

> Margaret McMillan, by substituting shelters in a garden for classrooms and a drab playground, demonstrated how the limitations imposed by [school] buildings and how this can be broken down. She believed that an open-air environment is of paramount importance for promoting the mental and physical development of children, and she proved that it is practicable to provide it in the very midst of a poor and crowded neighbourhood (p. 141).

At this time in history, the idea of the open-air nursery and careful consideration for young children's education reached the United States through the work of Abigail Adams Eliot, an American educator who became a leading authority on early childhood education after visiting England to study the growing nursery movement, which included studying with Margaret for three months in 1921. According to the Hadow Report (1933), "nursery schools, on the model of the McMillan School at Deptford, were established in considerable numbers in the United States after the close of the Great War" (p. 272).

In Britain, following World War II, the Education Act 1944 (Butler Act 1944) reiterated the need for nursery schools so that children under the age of five could benefit from the advantages offered by early-years education. The Education Act 1944 states that "a local education authority shall, in particular, have regard ... to the need for securing that provision is made for pupils who have not attained the age of five years by the provision of nursery schools ... " (p. 5). Although this provision was not compulsory for children under five years, its importance was acknowledged. The Butler Act went so far as to define what constitutes a nursery, saying "primary schools which are used mainly for the purpose of providing education for children who have attained the age of two years but have not attained the age of five years shall be known as nursery schools" (p. 6). Outlining what constitutes a nursery and ensuring that the local education authority would establish and maintain early-years education reiterated the importance placed on nursery education in the Hadow Report (1933).

In 1967, the Plowden Report was released, reiterating the need for and benefits of nursery education that the Hadow Report (1933) proffered. The Plowden Report examined the need to address deprivation through high-quality education and highlighted the advantages of nursery education. Reflecting the McMillan sisters' ethos of providing a well-designed, nurturing learning environment for children living in derivation, the Plowen Report stated that:

> part-time attendance at a nursery school is desirable for most children. It is even more so for children in socially deprived neighbourhoods. They need above all the verbal stimulus, the opportunities for constructive play, a more richly differentiated environment and the access to medical care that good nursery schools can provide (p. 63).

Additionally, as Margaret had hoped, the Plowden Report (1967) encouraged the development of nursery education to reach the socially deprived neighbourhoods that would most benefit from it. The report explicitly declares that "The expansion of nursery education should begin in the priority areas" (p. 67). The argument for nursery schools in the report goes on to name the McMillan sisters, saying:

> From 1907 it became the policy of the Board of Education to encourage the exclusion from school of children under five, who were often attending in surprisingly large numbers, unless special arrangements could be made for them. One effect was to stimulate the foundation of nursery schools by private effort. Rachel and Margaret McMillan were outstanding among the pioneers. Nursery schools first became eligible for grant in 1919 but growth has been slow, although the last war gave them a temporary boost (pp. 99–100).

Clearly, the McMillan sisters had an impact on the consideration and development of nursery education and its provision beyond their era of influence.

In 2000, the Qualifications and Curriculum Authority (QCA) and the Department for Education and Employment (DfEE) released Curriculum Guidance for the Foundation Stage—a comprehensive guide for practitioners working with young children. This document again reflects the ethos and considerations of the McMillan sisters, setting out guidelines for outstanding education for young children. Similar to the McMillans, the aim of this document was "to provide a high quality, integrated early education and childcare service for all who want it" (QCA Qualifications and Curriculum Authority, p. 3). Margaret McMillan was quite focused on making sure that teachers of young children were well educated and well informed about children's development. The Curriculum Guidance (2000) reflects this, saying:

> Effective education requires both a relevant curriculum and practitioners who understand and are able to implement the curriculum requirements. Effective education requires practitioners who understand that children develop rapidly during the early years—physically, intellectually, emotionally and socially (p. 14).

Similar to the Plowden Report (1967), the Curriculum Guidance (2000) emphasises the need for collaboration with families, stating that "Parents and practitioners should work together in an atmosphere of mutual respect within which children can have security and confidence" (p. 13). This resonates with the McMillan sisters' ideals for supporting families whose children were enrolled in the nursery by visiting them in their homes and providing needed services to improve their lives. The guidance goes on to say that "The significant adults to whom children relate during the foundation stage expand from the family to include the practitioners in early-years settings. Children, their parents and practitioners need to develop positive relationships based on trust" (p. 22). This tenet of trust was the driving force of the McMillan nursery and led to the community embracing the sisters and the nursery as their own.

Again echoing the Hadow Report (1933) and the philosophy of the McMillan sisters, the Curriculum Guidance (2000) clearly espouses the benefits and need for children's learning to take place outdoors:

> Outdoor activities allow children to have real experiences for example, of weather, of creatures in their natural environment and of the buildings that surround them. It allows them to work on a large scale, such as in construction, water play and mapping (p. 85).

The principles of the open-air nursery are reflected here, establishing that real experiences outside of an enclosed classroom offers children an ideal opportunity to learn and grow through enjoyment and challenge.

Looking at more contemporary guidance for young children's learning, the Tickell Report (Tickell 2011) encourages similar ideals to the McMillan sisters in addition to the abovementioned reports and guidance. It affirms "a strong start in the early years increases the probability of positive outcomes in later life; a weak foundation significantly increases the risk of later difficulties" (p. 8), similar to what Margaret McMillan promoted. The Tickell Report (Tickell 2011) also promotes the importance of communication and connections with families: "The most important influences on children's early development are those that come from home. Children benefit most when they experience the consistent support and presence of caring adults—carers, parents or other family members—from the earliest possible age" (Tickell 2011, p. 8). These partnerships help ensure the future of a child's educational experiences.

Currently, early-years education is guided by the Early Years Foundation Framework of 2017 (EYFS), which establishes standards for the learning, development and care of children from birth to 5 years of age. Throughout the document, play is emphasised, highlighting that "Play is essential for children's development, building their confidence as they learn to explore, to think about problems, and relate to others" (Department for Education 2017, p. 8). This document, echoing the McMillans' ideals about children's learning outdoors, clearly expresses the need for open-air learning, saying that "providers must provide access to an outdoor play area or, if that is not possible, ensure that outdoor activities are planned and taken on a daily basis" (Department for Education 2017, p. 30). Over 100 years after the open-air nursery was established, we still acknowledge the benefits of children engaging in outdoor experiences.

Parent partnerships play a significant role in young children's learning and development, and this is also a focus in the Department for Education (2017): "Practitioners should address any learning and development needs in partnership with parents and/or carers, and any relevant professionals" (p. 13). The framework clearly identifies the need for and importance of parent partnerships, stating that it seeks to provide "partnership working between practitioners and with parents and/or carers" (p. 5.), implying the need for trust between the adults who are the primary carers for young children. In a section outlining the learning and development requirements for young children, the framework defines what practitioners must do in order to work "in partnership with parents and/or carers, to promote the learning and development of all children in their care, and to ensure they are ready for school" (Department for Education 2017, p. 7).

In keeping with the work the McMillan sisters put into addressing young children living in poverty, the Labour Government (1997–2010) made early-years education a priority and released the Every Child Matters (ECM Every Child Matters) document, stating that they "increased the focus on prevention through the child poverty strategy, Sure Start, and our work to raise school standards" (p. 9). Additionally, similar to the McMillan sisters, the document acknowledged that "Parental involvement in education seems to be a more important influence than poverty, school environment and the influence of peers" (ECM Every Child Matters, p. 24). The ECM (Every Child Matters) also intends to "Tackle the key drivers of poor outcomes, including poverty, poor childcare and early years education, poor schooling and lack of access to health services" (p. 26). Recognising the need for access to health services reflects back to the health offices the McMillan sisters established even before opening the nursery.

An outcome of the Every Child Matters document was the establishment of Sure Start Children's Centres that echo the education services offered by the McMillan sisters. "Sure Start children's centres were designed to deliver a place in every community that would provide integrated care and services for young children and their families, with a particular focus on closing the achievement gap for children from disadvantaged backgrounds" (Bouchal and Norris 2012, p. 3). The idea that every community would benefit from a range of services offered in one centre mirrors the intentions of the McMillan sisters to provide care and education for children and their families. Similar to the sisters' nursery, Sure Start Centres were designed to be a "key mechanism for improving outcomes for young children, thereby reducing inequalities, and helping to bring an end to child poverty" (Bouchal and Norris 2012, p. 4). The nursery that the McMillan sisters opened eventually became a Sure Start Centre.

Although Sure Start Centres reflect the ethos of the McMillan sisters by making "an attempt to reshape local service provision in an area where services had been fragmented and where many different professions would have to work together" (Bouchal and Norris 2012, p. 18), by 2008, funding and support from the government were gradually withdrawn. There was, at this time, a shift in power that saw a coalition government take leadership, and austerity measures ensued. As a result, funding for Sure Start Centres was drastically curtailed, demonstrating that children are still held hostage to adult fortune much as they were during the lifetime of the McMillan sisters.

7. Conclusions

Because of their Christian Socialist ethos, the McMillan sisters eventually primarily focused on the nursery setting to create social change for children, families and the community. By creating change for impoverished children, it was hoped that they would break the cycle of poverty and live better lives, to which they were entitled. The McMillans' considered approach to young children from economically deprived backgrounds and their families pioneered a practice that still inspires early childhood education in the United Kingdom (UK). They dedicated their lives to plan "an appropriate environment for children and give them sunshine, fresh air and good food before they became rickety and diseased" (Stevinson 1954, p. 8). Mansbridge sums up Margaret's work and influence:

> She heard the call to work, she schemed, and planned and she succeeded. There is universal testimony, educational literature abounds with it, to the power of her redemptive action. Little children made straight, bounding into life, with bright eyes, attuned ears, sensitive touch and high spirits. The working mothers of Deptford, as they tell it, seem to be transformed; they speak of Margaret as one who did so much that she is, in the spirit still with them. The little children of the Nursery school returned to their homes as new creatures, inviting new conditions of feeding and treatment. All about them their elder sisters come from far, learn the magic and mystery of childhood, and go out to take other gardens in the midst of the slums. (Mansbridge 1932, pp. 82–83)

Margaret's dedication to improve the childhood experiences of the young children living in the squalor and deprivation of Deptford, London, led to the continuation of her ideals in contemporary early-years education. Her goal was for the nursery to be aspirational for children from socioeconomically deprived families, so the nursery was established to reflect the notion that:

> The garden is essential matter. Not the lessons or the pictures or the talk. The lessons and talk are about things seen in the garden, just as the best of all the paintings in the picture galleries are shadows of originals now available to the children of the open air. Ruskin declares that all the best books are written in the country ... Little children, as well as great writers, should be, if not in the country, at least in a place that is very like it ... If not in great space with moorland or forest and lakes, at least in sunny places, not in foul air and grimy congestion. (McMillan 1930, p. 4)

Having spent her own early years in the bucolic bliss of upstate New York, she dedicated her life and career to replicating some of those experiences for young children who, without her and the nursery, would, most likely, never have had nutritious food, self-directed activities and a large garden in which to learn, develop and grow. Margaret's work with the young children of Deptford led to the adoption of her ideals and practices in the British Independent Labour Party and Labour Party policies of her era. The ideals and ethos of the McMillan sisters continue to inform our approaches to teaching young children, as highlighted in the reports and policy that have and continue to inform the provision of early-years education.

Funding: This research received no external funding.

Conflicts of Interest: The author declares no conflict of interest.

References

BBC. 2019. The Boer War 1899–1902. Available online: https://www.bbc.com/bitesize/guides/zmgxsbk/revision/7 (accessed on 7 March 2019).

Bouchal, Petr, and Emma Norris. 2012. Implementing Sure Start Children's Centres. Available online: https://www.google.com/url?sa=t&rct=j&q=&esrc=s&source=web&cd=3&ved=2ahUKEwjQ6YH-zJ3jAhVWQUEAHf0ICg0QFjACegQIARAC&url=https%3A%2F%2Fwww.instituteforgovernment.org.uk%2Fsites%2Fdefault%2Ffiles%2Fpublications%2FImplementing%2520Sure%2520Start%2520Childrens%2520Centres%2520-%2520final_0.pdf&usg=AOvVaw1mx2ppOKH6by-GlOAt-ho_ (accessed on 7 March 2019).

Bradburn, Elizabeth. 1976. *Margaret McMillan: Portrait of a Pioneer*. London: Routledge.

Brehony, Kevin Joseph. *Progressive and Child-Centred Education*. London: Taylor and Francis.

Bruce, Tina. 1987. *Early Childhood Education*. London: Hodder Education.

Butler Act. 1944. *Education Act 1944 (7 and 8 Geo 6 c. 31)*. London: Longman.

Cunningham, Hugh. 2006. *The Invention of Childhood*. London: BBC Books.

Curriculum Guidance. 2000. *Curriculum guidance for the foundation stage*. London: Qualifications and Curriculum Authority, Available online: http://www.educationengland.org.uk/documents/foundationstage/2000-curriculum-guidance.pdf (accessed on 7 March 2019).

Department for Education. 2017. Statutory Framework for the Early Years Foundation Stage: Setting the Standards for Learning, Development and Care for Children from Birth to Five. Available online: https://webcache.googleusercontent.com/search?q=cache:nH7Hnk9TqpAJ:https://www.foundationyears.org.uk/files/2017/03/EYFS_STATUTORY_FRAMEWORK_2017.pdf+&cd=1&hl=en&ct=clnk&gl=uk (accessed on 23 January 2019).

ECM (Every Child Matters). 2003. Great Britain. HM Treasury. Available online: https://www.gov.uk/government/publications/every-child-matters (accessed on 23 January 2019).

Fried, Albert, and Richard M. Elman. 1969. *Charles Booth's London*. London: Hutchinson of London.

Giardiello, Patricia. 2014. *Pioneers in Early Childhood Education*. London: Routledge.

Griffin, Emma. 2014. Child Labour. Available online: https://www.bl.uk/romantics-and-victorians/articles/child-labour (accessed on 7 March 2019).

Hadow Report. 1933. *Infant and Nursery Schools*. London: HM Stationery Office.

Mansbridge, Albert. 1932. *Margaret McMillan Prophet and Pioneer*. London: J. M. Dent.

McMillan, Margaret. 1900. *Early Childhood*. London: S. Sonnenschein Co. Ltd.

McMillan, Margaret. 1917. *The Camp School*. London: George Allen & Unwin, Ltd.

McMillan, Margaret. 1930. *The Nursery School*. London: J. M. Dent & Sons.

McMillan, Margaret. 1927. *The Life of Rachel McMillan*. London: J. M. Dent & Sons, Ltd.

Plowden Report. 1967. *Children and their Primary Schools: A Report of the Central Advisory Council for Education (England)*. London: Her Majesty's Stationery Office.

QCA (Qualifications and Curriculum Authority). 2000. *Curriculum Guidance for the Foundation Stage*. London: QCA Publications, Available online: http://www.educationengland.org.uk/documents/foundationstage/2000-curriculum-guidance.pdf (accessed on 4 February 2019).

Ruskin, John. 1906. *The Library Edition of the Works of John Ruskin*. London: Smith, Elder & Co., vol. 17, pp. 405–9.

Steedman, Carolyn. 1990. *Childhood, Culture and Class in Britain: Margaret McMillan 1860–1931*. London: Virago Press.

Steele, Jess., ed. 1996. *The Streets of London: The Booth Notebooks—South East*. London: Deptford Forum Publishing Ltd.

Stevinson, Emma. 1954. *Margaret McMillan: Prophet and Pioneer*. London: University of London Press.

Tickell, Dame C. 2011. *The Early Years: Foundations for Life, Health and Learning: An Independent Report on the Early Years Foundation Stage to Her Majesty's Government*. London: Department for Education.

Williams, Anthony Alan John. 2016. Christian Socialism as a Political Ideology. Available online: https://livrepository.liverpool.ac.uk/3001797/1/200514195_Mar2016.pdf (accessed on 7 March 2019).

© 2019 by the author. Licensee MDPI, Basel, Switzerland. This article is an open access article distributed under the terms and conditions of the Creative Commons Attribution (CC BY) license (http://creativecommons.org/licenses/by/4.0/).

Article

Does Early Childhood Education in England for the 2020s Need to Rediscover Susan Isaacs: Child of the Late Victorian Age and Pioneering Educational Thinker?

Philip Hood

School of Education, University of Nottingham, Nottingham NG7 2RD, UK; philip.hood1@nottingham.ac.uk

Received: 30 April 2019; Accepted: 10 July 2019; Published: 11 July 2019

Abstract: Since the nineteenth century, the history of childhood has been inextricably linked to the history of schooling. Throughout the period of state-provided schooling, the approach to teaching the youngest children, originally from five but currently usually from three years old, has been contentious. This article looks at Susan Isaacs as a major figure in the shaping of views about early childhood education and thus in the history of contemporary childhood. It surveys her rather special position as someone who was herself a child in the urban late Victorian school system when schooling became compulsory for all, and who later combined radical innovation in the combination of educational theory and practice. She experienced for a period the running of a small experimental primary school on a daily basis, yet also engaged in high level academic research and writing which was founded on psychological, educational and, unusually for the time, observational principles. She thus provided evidence-based thinking for policy making at a crucial point in England's educational history (The 1944 Education Act). Her early life, her neighbourhood as shown by the 1901 census and the educational significance of her position on the value of assessment through detailed observation are discussed within the overall context of the last one hundred and thirty years of educational change. This reveals the principles which formed during her childhood and which teachers who work with young children share now even though these are challenged by current government policy. This article focuses on educational policy in England, as the other countries of the UK have at times evolved separate structures for their school systems.

Keywords: early childhood education; Susan Isaacs; urban Lancashire demographic sample 1901

---

1. Introduction

1.1. Susan Isaacs-Key Facts

Susan Isaacs lived from 1885 to 1948 and is noted for a range of varied activity: her many writings including two major field-based studies (Isaacs 1930, 1933); her role as head teacher under the directorship of Geoffrey Pyke of the experimental Maltings House School in Cambridge during the 1920s; and her academic role as head of the child development department at the University of London Institute of Education from 1933. She contributed to the 1932 Hadow Report on Infant and Nursery Schools and to the framing of the 1944 Education Act which has, since that time, sat at the heart of the education system in England and to an extent determined its parameters, rather as the National Health Service has been defined by the core principles of its launch in 1948. As her obituary in *Nature* (1948, p. 881) summarised (my italics):

> 'Few can have had a greater influence in our time on the upbringing and education of children; indeed, the modern trend towards full recognition of the *human* aspect of nursery school and subsequent education owes much to her work.'

Susan Isaacs is the subject of this article because she drew from her own experience, period of study and working life, from starting school in 1890 through to her death in 1948, a coherent philosophy about early childhood education (ECE) which on one level offers a remarkable continuity through to the present day, but which on another level is the source of divergent views and conflicting policies. Her work was cited in the Plowden report of 1967 and was represented also through her husband Nathan Isaacs' contributions to that very influential publication. It, like her work as a whole, lies at the heart of the debate about the nature of early childhood education in the twenty-first century.

1.2. The Current Context of Early Childhood Education

The first section of this article looks at the British attitude to 'childhood' and 'schooling' as it developed from the introduction of compulsory education; as part of this we will see that there is a marked tendency for childhood to become secondary to schooling and to a preparation for adulthood.

Childhood is a construct which throughout history has been shaped and reshaped by adults, principally adults in power (Valkanova 2014). Some of the roles children have had laid upon them have been determined by pragmatic considerations with the interests of adults or society as paramount. This is as true in the twenty-first century as it was in the late nineteenth. The claims of government policy about improving the educational standards of all children are essentially consistent through that period of time and yet the context for such ambitions has changed rapidly between 1880 and 2019. Some of the debate about the nature of and purpose of childhood might be initiated by philosophers or other types of educators, but at an everyday level it is the family and immediate community which inevitably sets out the reality of what it is to be a child. Early childhood education (ECE) is an aspect of the nature of childhood which since the late Victorian times has gradually encompassed all children from the age of three, four or five years. The current structure in England divides the system at five years. Before that, the Early Years Foundation Stage covers ages birth to five with its own framework and curriculum; from five, the National Curriculum has specifications which cover learning to the age of fourteen with examination syllabuses taking that forward to sixteen and eighteen. In ECE, an international dimension in ideas appears to have been an accepted aspect of policy making until the last twenty years in England; for example, the significant and influential Plowden Report of 1967, which cited Isaacs' work, emphasised approaches which originated in the thinking of the swiss psychologist Piaget (1936). Recently, however, the influence of how things are actually done abroad has lessened significantly as a divide between research and practice has opened up. Under the three Labour governments, beginning in 1997 and the subsequent Coalition and Conservative governments up to the time of writing, England especially has increasingly set out its educational course separately and with an introvert focus, preferring to identify and 'solve' its problems from within. Where policy makers reference other systems, for example Singapore (see critique by Hogan 2014) and Finland (Hart 2017), the core structures and belief-systems they build upon are often virtually ignored and, especially in the case of Finland, cherry-picked even when those cherries are a tiny element of the recipe.

This was not always the case and in the field of ECE from the early twentieth century, both theoretical and experiential thinking from Europe, for example from Froebel, Piaget, Montessori and from the USA, e.g., Dewey were commonly discussed. But currently, increasingly, even the pool of what constitutes 'from within' has shrunk as the twenty-first century has progressed. The Education Secretary from 2010 to 2014, Michael Gove, denounced in a series of statements (e.g., The Daily Telegraph 2013, 24 March 2013) as 'enemies of promise' education academics, local education authorities and 'militant' striking teachers. There was also a disdain for 'experts' (Jackson and Ormerod 2017), a role for which Isaacs was clearly admired according to the Obituary in *Nature* (1948). This divide in who has authority in education constitutes a dispute about the nature and role of childhood now as surely as in the late nineteenth century when with the new emphasis on compulsory schooling, children were seen as in a separate stage of life and not merely mini-adults waiting for work and adulthood. Yet, at the same time, a good education is of course designed to lead to a usefulness to society. Valkanova (2014) has shown how across history childhood, as a concept, has itself been constructed to fit with the power dynamics of each age. She points to how in the early twentieth century the concepts of the progressive child (with its self-constructed identity) and of the normalised child (seen through the parameters of standardised testing) both grew to popularity. We might say that both survive now in the opposing views of the need for the child to be ready for school or the school to be ready for the child.

The new National Curriculum (DfE 2013) replaced the reformed (but cancelled) 2009 version (DCSF 2009) and could be said to be its polar opposite; the 2013 programme emphasises narrowly bounded subjects with a strong emphasis on core skills of Literacy and Numeracy, as opposed to a broader, more integrated domain-based structure that Rose had articulated in his 2009 report. In a special edition of the journal *Education 3-13*, Duncan (2010, p. 342) in her editorial, writing about the Rose Review and also the previous Cambridge Review of Primary Education (see Cambridge Review of Primary Education 2010 for an overview), stated (her italics):

> 'Several of the proposals set out in both reviews have the potential to begin the process of constructing a curriculum which is more responsive to the ways in which *children* believe they best learn. The immense care taken by both reviews to acknowledge and take account of the voices of children, parents, local communities, head teachers, teachers as well as researchers and educationalists has produced a set of recommendations in which a wide constituency of stakeholders have played an important part.'

The Gove declarations about enemies of promise and experts give an insight as to why the incoming Coalition government cancelled the new curriculum before it had even been introduced.

Leading up to the two new versions of curriculum, from 1997 there were, through the twin prongs of, firstly, the original National Curriculum (which had only been launched in 1988) and its offspring The Primary Strategy (1999–2010) and, secondly, a rigorous inspection regime, a very heightened concrete focus on 'standards'. This produced, in that period, comparison tables between schools, the grading of schools, teachers and even individual lessons and a relentless pressure on headteachers and their staff to narrow the curriculum priorities to English and mathematics at the expense of all other subject disciplines. From 2007, Teacher Education courses have been inspected specifically on their training for the teaching of reading and how far it meets the prescriptive government approach centred on the use of systematic synthetic phonics (SSP). The standards-led focus has in the last couple of years spread to early childhood education with the publication of a report, Bold Beginnings, from OFSTED (the schools inspection agency) (OFSTED 2017). In this report, schools are urged to make the Reception Year (children aged 4–5 years) more formal with a heightened emphasis on Literacy and Numeracy and especially on the use of SSP for the early teaching of reading. This is designed to lead in to the revised 2013 National Curriculum at Key Stage 1 (5–7 years) which raised expectations from previous iterations. Similarly, the government is introducing from 2020 a compulsory baseline test for children entering the Reception year which will eventually be used to compare progress between the ages of four and eleven. Children spend at least six hours a day, thirty-nine weeks a year in school and whether from two years old if they access the recent government extension to schooling, from three years old if they attend a Nursery class or from four if they start at Reception level, school defines a major part of their waking childhood and they are 'measured, throughout the period from starting school until eleven years in a variety of education-based tests and health screenings. We can see therefore that childhood and schooling are inextricably linked.

2. Late Victorian State Schooling

It is not possible to make a realistic comparison of curriculum between 1890 and 2019 since there was no national Curriculum in Victorian times, but clearly reading and writing and arithmetic were the staple diet then, as they are now with the current strong focus on the disciplines of English and Mathematics. Of course, between then and now, the resources for teaching, the training of teachers, the cultural expectations of school, the identification of pupil need, the psychological understanding of development and cognition are all worlds apart. The concern for standards has been ever-present from the mid-Victorian period, although it is more difficult to be accurate about the changing motivation for the pressures this brings. For example, when, in their historical review of education, Nutbrown and Clough (2014, p. 7) state:

> 'By 1862, the Revised Code was introduced whereby grants were awarded to elementary schools, depending upon the achievement of their pupils. Forster's Education Act of 1870 established school boards in areas where there was a lack of elementary school provision [,]'

We might maintain that the thrust of those policies, despite their enforcement ethos, was the widening of school access and improvement of young children's life prospects and a more egalitarian view of how society should develop. According to Shuttleworth (2010) the child began to be seen as the bearer of the future rather than as a commodity or mini-adult. By 1890, the payment by results policy was questioned and although not immediately ended we can see that as schooling had become compulsory, a more collective societal responsibility for education was emerging. In fact, following the Acts of 1870 (the first major Education act), the Factory Act of 1878 which prohibited child labour before the age of ten, the Education Act of 1880 (when school attendance between the ages of 5–10 became compulsory) and 1882 when the Mundella Code emphasised enlightened teaching methods and a variety of subjects, schooling gradually became the norm for the majority of young children. Schools had been inspected for some time and Arnold who served for many years as a school inspector wrote about the tensions of the sometimes conflicting views of government, schools, the Church (who ran so many schools) the inspectorate itself (see Campbell 2013) and was thus contentious then as now. Following the Education Acts and the advent of compulsory schooling, the inspection framework became an annual event and the School Boards also visited to evaluate whether any grants should be paid. In this way, there was an attempt to monitor a fledgling national system and to establish some norms of quality in matters of attendance and standards. The terms used by inspectors, according to one Midlands school for which we have an overview of daily log book data, centred on the intelligence of the pupils, the efficiency of the schools, the discipline and tone of the classrooms (Hodge 2008).

Mixed age teaching was still very common in late Victorian times because there was often a single teacher in a school so pupils of four to nine or eleven were routinely in the same class. In some urban areas, the headteacher would have an assistant teacher, who could be unqualified and there was also the use of pupil-teachers in some cases. In the Midlands school case (Hodge 2008), there was segregation of the sexes rather than of age levels above the infant stage. At one point (1890), we see a staff of four (a headteacher, assistant teacher, pupil-teacher and a monitor) between them teaching 180 girls across seven school years. Clearly, here it was possible for children to 'go missing' in the classroom as close scrutiny of attention and work was highly problematic. Actual school attendance was monitored, however, and schools had to produce statistics for the annual inspections. At that school, one School Board visit (in 1902) questioned the staffing levels as not being generous enough and warned about the withdrawal of the grant (Hodge 2008).

Although the concern for 'standards' is therefore not new, there is a difference between a time when compulsory education for the benefit of all seemed a noble aim to work for and the present day when an enormous amount of research has interrogated the nature of child development, child psychology and pedagogies have blossomed with the myriad types of artefacts, media and technology that the twentieth century and the opening years of the twenty-first have produced. In 2013 in the lead-up to the publication of the new National Curriculum an attributed BBC report (Coughlan 2013) stated: 'Michael Gove promised to rid the curriculum of "vapid happy talk" and ensure pupils had a structured "stock of knowledge"'. The rhetoric currently is that all children should be able to succeed equally and it is the debate about what qualities really constitute the best approach to education for all that is currently so contentious. It is in the education of the youngest children that the debate truly rages and many teachers of the 21st Century feel that the potential of so much developmental work centred around childhood and children's real learning needs is currently ignored. One social media example of this is a closed Facebook group with over 40,000 members which is dedicated to maintaining a child-centred focus for 2–5-year olds in school. The tone of this group is very much one (in equal amounts) of positive pedagogical sharing and frustration at the external pressures on schools to comply with what is seen as a narrow government policy. As we have tried to show here, the view of schooling for this young age group certainly defines a large part of the actual childhood of those passing through the system although the policy makers conveniently avoid any definition of childhood, merely emphasising the need for standards to rise and social mobility to be effected. As Morgan, the then Minister of Education, said in the DfE Strategy document (2015)

> 'My vision is to provide world-class education and care that allows every child and young person to reach his or her potential, regardless of background … … Children only get one childhood and one chance at their education, so there is a real urgency in our need to deliver'
> (DfE 2016, pp. 3–4)

In fact, that document (DfE Strategy 2015–2020) only contains one occurrence of the word childhood and it comes, very much conflated with the idea of education at the end of the introduction.

The fact that in the late nineteenth century there were financial rewards for schools if they reached certain standards does indicate a similar pressure on a system to comply with whatever it was that inspector and school Boards advised; it does also demonstrate the historical precedent of what might currently influence heads and teachers to find the most efficient way of reaching targets without necessarily considering the children's diverse preferences, needs or contexts. It is probably fair to say that just as society in the late Victorian period was structured around quite rigid hierarchies and an expectation that the population in general would respect these boundaries and authorities, so were schools. Whereas currently, rebellion or at least non-compliance is a part of society which few would pretend is absent or should simply be crushed, that was perhaps more a feature of the thinking of the 1890s. A small-scale 'rebel' from the period who became a key figure in the framing of the debate about the nature and most appropriate model of early childhood education in the UK was Susan Sutherland Isaacs (1885–1948). Isaacs was born and grew up in Turton, which lies immediately to the north of Bolton in Lancashire.

3. The Environment in Turton

Turton is a district to the North of Bolton, where Isaacs' father edited the newspaper, the Bolton Journal and Guardian. The area is described on the internet site British History Online (https://www.british-history.ac.uk/vch/lancs/vol5/pp273-281) in these terms, relating to 1911:

> 'There are numerous cotton mills, print works, bleach works, dye works, and quarries. The land is chiefly in pasture. The Egerton spinning mills were formerly worked by a powerful water wheel. There is a disused paper mill at Chapeltown.'

The family lived in houses around Bromley Cross which is and was a part of the township close to the edge of the Bolton urban area. The 1901 census for Turton was completed in two halves and the eastern half centring on Bromley Cross contained a population of 1611 spread across some two hundred records. Clearly the infant mortality rate of the time was greater in industrial urban centres, especially in mining and textile areas (Jaadla and Reid 2017) and the records on any one date mask the past infant and child deaths in each family. The census reported two hundred and twenty-two children of sixteen or under living in that part of the town which would have been Isaacs' immediate community. Around fifty-three percent of the households included children and therefore, perhaps surprisingly, a relatively high proportion (around forty-seven per cent) were all-adult households, either with predominantly older or middle-aged residents and occasionally a younger couple without children at that point. Excepting farms where the population was more varied, only ten households included servants. No child under twelve was shown as at work and only two of nine of that age had an occupation listed on the census. However, from thirteen up to sixteen years, the majority were at work. At thirteen, the balance was close with nine of seventeen working, but at fourteen and fifteen the great majority had an occupation listed (eleven of twelve at fourteen and fifteen of seventeen at fifteen). There were fewer sixteen-year olds on the census register but only one of the ten listed was not shown as working: that is Susan Isaacs, bearing her birth name Susan Sutherland Fairhurst. The occupations of these forty-six children included a strong majority carrying out a range of jobs at either the local bleach works or cotton mill (usually following a family employment pattern); but the figure also included dressmakers, labourers, an errand boy, a sawyer, a clerk, a wheelwright apprentice, and a confectioner (possibly a sweet shop assistant). From a census, it is of course impossible to know whether the younger children were attending school regularly and that they were not sometimes employed in their family's line of work or working to help keep the house. What we see from these statistics is that Isaacs would have been conscious of her different position from that of the majority of her counterpart and from the wider cohorts immediately above and below her age which would have been linked to her older and younger siblings.

Isaacs had, in some ways, a privileged childhood and learning formed a strong part of that as the large family was cultured and creative. But her life was not without its traumas. Her mother died when she was six years old after a long illness following the birth of her younger sister. Her father remarried quite quickly and this involved a woman who had been in the house for a time nursing his wife. Biographies make much of the fact that the young Susan mentioned that relationship innocently to her mother just before she died (Gardner 1969) and

> 'according to Susan's later recollection, someone came and led her away from her mother's bedside. Her last memory of her mother was of her mother's white face wearing an expression of deep distress that she herself had caused.' (Graham 2009, p. 37)

The incident is held to show that this demonstrated her strong desire always to tell the truth and to report what she saw. This clinical objectivity formed a strong part of her later work in education although according to all accounts of her life she was certainly not without emotion or humour.

Isaacs' childhood in the home, as noted above, was not always happy and neither was her schooling. She attended a Methodist school from five and then a relatively new secondary school from when she was twelve. This required an entrance examination and was much larger than the elementary school. Summarising her educational experience, Graham (2009, p. 49) writes:

> 'One might have hoped that for a child suffering so much grief at home, school would have been a compensating experience. This was certainly not the case as far as her elementary school was concerned; here she was teased and found no pleasure in learning. This school was, by comparison with others of the day in the same city, poorly run. The teaching was regarded as of low quality and some of her teachers found difficulty in keeping order. Her secondary grammar-type school was more demanding and stimulating, but even here she was not happy. She remained a difficult and troublesome girl.'

The linking from her own childhood into her later educational work and writing is demonstrated by an article she wrote later. According to Graham (2009, p. 44) she referred to a girl (whom he identifies as almost certainly herself), who:

> '"throughout her school years was characterised by obstinacy, noisiness, insubordination, seeking after boys, occasional stealing". At seven years "she ate chalk ... She used in school to blow her nose very loudly in order to annoy a woman teacher whom she much admired and loved"'

The household which was cultured, athletic and involved much musical activity, was 'lined with bookcases' (Gardner 1969, p. 31) which were according to Graham (2009, p. 34) 'not just on revivalist religion, but on politics, the arts, history, travel and, of course, sport.' These topics represented the context of her father's occupation as a journalist working in Bolton and his close adherence to his Methodist faith which also meant the children had Sundays busy with church activity. Not only were the books very varied but so, according to a family friend (Gardner 1969), were the family's activities which were often based outdoors. The surroundings combined the industrial with the natural and in conversations with her biographer (Gardner 1969) Isaacs commented on the attraction in later life when she returned to the area both of the grimy houses and mills and of the nobility of the moors and the charmingly wooded valleys. Clearly, she was not a child who sat indoors, read and saw no-one which gives a rationale to the argument that her origins and experienced strongly underpinned her later thinking about the needs of young children and education.

One of Isaacs' older sisters is shown in the census as working as a school teacher and was probably a pupil-teacher at Susan's school in Bolton at one point, but by 1901 none of the brothers whom she valued as intellectual companions, was still living at home. Susan herself was to have periods of teaching or tutoring between the time she left school and starting higher education (see below). The pattern of the neighbourhood, that from twelve years upwards children quickly abandoned school and started working, the majority in challenging factory environments which involved potentially harmful chemicals, would certainly have made her count herself fortunate and is likely to have formed a view about the value of education which she had already benefited from and was to continue as she moved eventually into higher education. She talked about this to her biographer Gardner who cites her (Gardner 1969, p. 35):

> 'I remember periods of pinching and even of famine among the cotton workers ... There was no unemployment benefit, no insurance, no general social responsibility for starving children, and skilled men could not find work. But fellow feeling was strong and direct ... the chapel or the church called upon the lucky ones in half-time, if not in full-time work to pool their resources for the more needy. Many families who attended the Wesleyan Chapel in my own village deprived themselves for a week or a month of all butter on their own bread or sugar in their tea and paid the savings into the common fund for the help of their less fortunate friends.'

But at sixteen, although not shown to have an occupation in the 1901 census, she was ironically, not actually in school as her father had withdrawn her at the age of fourteen or fifteen (accounts vary) to counter her developing agnosticism (Gardner 1969) and so her education continued autonomously before she finally attended higher education via a route at Manchester University which was intended to prepare students for teacher training. This course introduced her to the work of Dewey and Froebel which were to inform her thinking about education greatly by the time she opened the Cambridge based Maltings House School in 1924. She was recommended to transfer to a full degree-level course and after an intervention from an academic which convinced her father he should finance this, she gained entry to Philosophy in which she subsequently gained a First Class degree. She had had to study very rapidly two foreign languages to achieve the entry requirement and managed to reach a sufficient level in both German and Ancient Greek partly alone, partly with the help of a family member. Not only did she demonstrate very high intellectual ability but also substantial originality of thought; this rare combination was no doubt founded in her experience of taking a mediocre school education and combining it with the rich family culture and then the opportunities which the Manchester courses offered. Having such qualities ensured she was noticed and she was subsequently offered a scholarship at Newnham College Cambridge where she began to study Psychology. Her subsequent activity as detailed below suggests that she always carried her early experience with her.

4. Isaacs' Developing Theories

After her time at Cambridge, Isaacs became heavily involved in and influenced by the emerging psychoanalytical theories which came from Freud and his school. These provided a foundation for the way in which she observed the children at the Maltings House School; she launched the institution in Cambridge as an experimental school with its proprietor in 1924 after connections between the two were made by a mutual acquaintance within the psychoanalysis community. Among Isaacs' major influences, importantly in the sense that she acknowledged but also critiqued them, were Dewey, Piaget and Montessori. Dewey had himself addressed the theories of Froebel, who is usually regarded as the originator of the kindergarten style of early childhood education through establishing a laboratory school in Chicago and so a direct line can be traced between the approaches he carried out and how Isaacs decided to run her own institution. Froebel had in turn learned from Pestalozzi, a disciple of Rousseau, so a connection back to the eighteenth century was established which drew in long discussions about both childhood and education. The Stanford Encyclopedia of Philosophy (2017) characterises Rousseau's theories of education as centring on the need to protect and develop a child's natural goodness and that the educational process should be that:

> 'The child is not told what to do or think but is led to draw its own conclusions as a result of its own explorations, the context for which has been carefully arranged.'

It is interesting that we can trace the particular thread of thinking about early childhood education back by around two hundred and fifty years, note its role at a point approaching a hundred years ago and still see the issue as a matter of debate in the current educational system. This is not about the essential goodness of a child, as we have seen Isaacs' own self-assessment countering that line of thought, but about the nature of deep learning. The Rousseau method in its most simple iteration, as outlined above, still has the presence of a teacher, but one who creates a learning environment and then truly facilitates from the side. The talent for 'careful arrangement' is crucial as it is a deep pedagogic knowledge that enables that to be done most effectively. It requires a certain amount of bravery to wait in the confidence that the learning environment *will* truly enable progress in terms of deeper understanding and more embedded skills rather than in terms of content memorisation. As we saw earlier, the current debates in the ECE arena stem from exactly this divide in the view as to what the true purposes of early education are. In this sense, we might say that Isaacs was in tune with the thinking from central and northern Europe and from the U via her tutor at Manchester, Grace Owen, in a way that is not prevalent now amongst policy makers, although ironically it is far more understood by teachers than was the case in the 1920s when she ran Maltings House.

Isaacs' thinking developed directly from the twin sources of her reading of progressive sources and her own longitudinal observation at the school and these two separate but related interactive strands culminated in the two publications (Isaacs 1930, 1933) on Intellectual and Social Growth respectively. In these, she reflected on how children learn and also crucially what the curriculum should contain:

> 'For me, the school has two main sorts of function: (a) to provide for the development of the child's own bodily and social skills and means of expression; and (b) to open the facts of the external world (the real external world, that is, not the school "subjects") to him [sic] in such a way that he can seize and understand them.' (Isaacs 1930, p. 20)

She continues (Isaacs 1930, pp. 20–21) 'This view has long been associated with the name and work of John Dewey.' Dewey (1899, 1902, 1916) had written three very influential works regarded as the foundations of progressive education and in turn had been influenced by the thinking of Froebel (1888) (regarding the value of learning through play and the nature of an early childhood kindergarten ethos which he created through running his own kindergarten), which informed Dewey's experimental school at the University of Chicago at the turn of the twentieth century and thereafter. Given Isaacs' decision to use close longitudinal observation at the Maltings House School we see the rise to prominence of practice-oriented theory generation. Her referencing of and discussion of Piaget's work demonstrates her close attention to contemporary thinking as Piaget's 'Language and Thought of the Child' was first published in English in 1926 and Isaacs uses his material and critiques it in the 1930 publication 'Intellectual Growth in Young Children'. Crucially, she critiques Piaget's explanation of development through his developmental stages as not simply biological maturation but a process which contains social factors where the:

> 'process of socialisation is gradual and continuous ... ... and that the "social instincts" which appear more marked at seven to eight years undoubtedly have, at any rate in part, an individual history ... ' (Isaacs 1930, p. 79)

This possibly anticipates the more social-constructivist approach of Vygotsky (1978) which was contemporary to Isaacs' life but not translated from the original Russian until the late 1970s. For Isaacs, it was important to establish a naturalistic learning environment and self-directed play as the basis for her rigorous scientific observations of children and to capture everything they said and did. This accords with the Vygotskian emphasis on learning first in a social context through dialogue with others and the importance of language for learning. It also highlights that children develop individually and on a path that is not necessarily like that of others. Current practice in early childhood education in England is centred around close observation as the main method of identifying both children's development and the most appropriate next steps in their learning. This is both at an individual setting level where adults use the method on a daily basis while interacting with children as individuals or small groups and in materials or approaches which have been developed as instruments, such as the Leuven Scales (Laevers 1994). Isaacs is undoubtedly a pioneer in this approach in the English context and her direct legacy is perhaps most clearly seen in this aspect of early childhood education.

She clearly sets out the observational approach in some detail in the Introduction to the 1930 volume (Isaacs 1930) but also admits that a purely objective observer does not exist and that children inevitably respond to being observed. She acknowledges observer bias too, citing the example of a psychologist who observed his own children and was not able to extricate his own parental approach from his observational notes or see that his views impacted on what he was observing. With these insights we can say that it is reasonable to infer from Isaacs' writings about child development that her unconscious starting point is her own life experience combined with the very various learning that had followed with philosophy, psychology and psychoanalysis all deeply interrogated. Gardner (1969, p. 19) who talked to Isaacs many times as part of constructing the biography noted details she told her about her early education and concluded:

'Perhaps such experiences were the beginning of her deep conviction that learning is one of the ways in which we achieve stability and happiness, and that young children need to be taught in ways which they can understand.'

Isaacs reflected deeply on the twin areas of pedagogy and curriculum, drawing in the philosophies of child-centred educationalists as well as the rich observational material that she generated daily at the school and, also in her Introduction (Isaacs 1930, p. 21) discussed the ways in which school should arrive at its curriculum content: (original italics)

'We have been content to apply out new psychological knowledge of *how* the child learns, to the ways of getting him to learn the old things. We have not used it to enrich our understanding of *what* he needs to learn, nor of what experiences the school should bring to him.'

Earlier in the chapter (Isaacs 1930, p. 19):

'It is, for instance, so much easier from the point of view of space, of staffing and equipment, to keep the children relatively inactive and to "teach" them, than it is to arrange for them to "find out".'

Both of these citations appear to arise not just from what she knew happened around her in the average school but also from her own childhood. As we have seen earlier, she herself had had varied but not especially positive experiences at her two different schools but then crucially it was her experience of self-started, self-managed independent learning, where learning by doing alongside autonomous selection of reading material was very much the pattern of her daily life that appears to have been crucial in giving practical expression to the reading she had done at Manchester, Cambridge and thereafter.

5. Conclusions

We began by noting the interconnectedness of a view of childhood and a view of early childhood education. The former should logically inform the latter but a survey of current education policy suggests that the two are seen as separate, even unrelated. Isaacs experienced what she judged as an unsatisfactory education with a lack of emphasis on individual capacities, a lack of linking to the real world and a lack of pedagogical creativity. Her intensively detailed observations of young children's learning activity at the experimental school demonstrate that all of those qualities were matters to be considered in a brave approach which many might describe as risk-taking, but which Isaacs appears not to have feared. Her conviction that one needs to start from the child as Fisher (2013) more recently expressed it, and her strong belief in her ability to observe objectively and to make critical sense of what she saw appeared vindicated by the attainment of the children from Maltings House School as they progressed beyond it. She states (Isaacs 1930, p. 110) that from the schools the pupils moved to came reports commenting that they were: 'remarkable for their intelligence and adaptability' and that 'they are so very eager to learn.' There may be a difference of scale between a small experimental school and a vast education system but we should always remember that each four-year old has a single classroom and a single educational experience which can shape a future.

Isaacs' view of education was not laissez-faire. She highlighted the importance of learning but saw childhood as containing the natural desire to do so. She appears to have devoted an enormous energy to the 'careful arrangement' of the environment which attuned to Rousseau's views so long before. Now, at a time when childhood is theoretically safeguarded for so much longer than at previous points in history, we could perhaps learn from Isaacs' desire to unite the two concepts of a protected childhood with an exciting and creative education which builds understanding, skills and the capacity for independence. Isaacs' early life taken all together appears to have given her that portfolio of experiences, some happy, some traumatic, some frustrating, but it required an enormous amount of autonomous effort from her to counteract the more negative aspects. She extracted from that ways to ensure children did not need to wait so long and work so hard to reach the benefits of a carefully arranged learning environment. We should also heed that iteration of 'promise' and see in it a rationalised challenge to the prevailing policy view that to ensure that all children progress further we need to begin more formal teaching earlier. The clash between the disparate views on ECE should be given the Isaacs lens which was centred on rigorous, research informed close observation of real children engaged in the learning process. In that way, a policy which builds on the full learning of the last one hundred and thirty years could be adopted with confidence by the profession as a whole.

Funding: This research received no external funding.

Conflicts of Interest: The author declares no conflict of interest.

References

Cambridge Review of Primary Education. 2010. Available online: https://www.robinalexander.org.uk/wp-content/uploads/2012/05/CPR-final-report-briefing.pdf (accessed on 26 March 2019).

Campbell, Kate. 2013. Culture, Politics and Arnold Revisited: The Government Inspector, Disinterestedness and 'The Function of Criticism'. *Journal of Victorian Culture* 18: 230–45. [CrossRef]

Coughlan, Sean. 2013. Gove Sets Out 'Core Knowledge' Curriculum Plans. Available online: https://www.bbc.co.uk/news/education-21346812 (accessed on 8 July 2019).

DCSF. 2009. Review of the Primary Curriculum. Available online: http://www.educationengland.org.uk/documents/pdfs/2009-IRPC-final-report.pdf (accessed on 25 March 2019).

Dewey, John. 1899. *The School and Society*. Chicago: University of Chicago Press.

Dewey, John. 1902. *The Child and the Curriculum*. Chicago: University of Chicago Press.

Dewey, John. 1916. Democracy and Education: An Introduction to the Philosophy of Education. New York: Macmillan.

DfE. 2013. National Curriculum. Available online: https://assets.publishing.service.gov.uk/government/uploads/system/uploads/attachment_data/file/425601/PRIMARY_national_curriculum.pdf (accessed on 27 March 2019).

DfE. 2016. DfE Strategy 2015–2020. Available online: https://assets.publishing.service.gov.uk/government/uploads/system/uploads/attachment_data/file/508421/DfE-strategy-narrative.pdf (accessed on 1 April 2019).

Duncan, Diane. 2010. The Rose Review of the English primary curriculum. *Education* 38: 341–343. [CrossRef]

Fisher, Julie. 2013. *Starting from the Child*. Milton Keynes: Open University Press.

Froebel, Friedrich. 1888. *Autobiography of Friedrich Froebel*. Translated by Emily Michaelis, and H. Keatley Moore. London: Swan Sonnenschein.

Gardner, Dorothy E. M. 1969. *Susan Isaacs. The first Biography*. London: Methuen.

Graham, Philip. 2009. *Susan Isaacs: A Life Freeing the Minds of Children*. London: Routledge.

Hart, John. 2017. Available online: https://www.theguardian.com/teacher-network/2017/aug/09/worlds-best-school-system-trust-teachers-education-finland (accessed on 27 March 2019).

Hodge, P. T. 2008. The History of Kensington School 1886–1957. Unpublished manuscript.

Hogan, David. 2014. Available online: http://theconversation.com/why-is-singapores-school-system-so-successful-and-is-it-a-model-for-the-west-22917 (accessed on 27 March 2019).

Isaacs, Susan. 1930. *Intellectual Growth in Young Children*. London: Methuen.

Isaacs, Susan. 1933. *Social Development in Young Children*. London: Methuen.

Jaadla, Hannaliis, and Alice Reid. 2017. The Geography of Early Childhood Mortality in England and Wales, 1881–1911. Available online: https://www.demographic-research.org/volumes/vol37/58/37-58.pdf (accessed on 30 March 2019).

Jackson, Helen, and Paul Ormerod. 2017. Was Michael Gove Right? Have We Had Enough of Experts? Available online: https://www.prospectmagazine.co.uk/magazine/michael-gove-right-about-experts-not-trust-them-academics-peer-review (accessed on 27 March 2019).

Laevers, Ferre, ed. 1994. *The Leuven Involvement Scale for Young Children. (Manual and Video) Experiential Education Series, No. 1*. Leuven: Centre for Experiential Education.

Nature. 1948. Dr. Susan Isaacs, C.B.E. *Nature* 162: 881. [CrossRef]

Nutbrown, Cathy, and Peter Clough. 2014. *Early Childhood Education: History, Philosophy and Experience*. London: Sage.

OFSTED. 2017. Bold Beginnings: The Reception Curriculum in a Sample of Good and Outstanding Primary Schools. Available online: https://assets.publishing.service.gov.uk/government/uploads/system/uploads/attachment_data/file/663560/28933_Ofsted_-_Early_Years_Curriculum_Report_-_Accessible.pdf (accessed on 27 March 2019).

Piaget, Jean. 1936. *Origins of Intelligence in the Child*. London: Routledge & Kegan Paul.

Shuttleworth, Sally. 2010. *The Mind of the Child: Child Development in Literature, Science, and Medicine, 1840–1900*. Oxford: OUP.

Stanford Encyclopedia of Philosophy. 2017. Jean Jacques Rousseau. Available online: https://plato.stanford.edu/entries/rousseau/#Educ (accessed on 1 April 2019).

The Daily Telegraph. 2013. Available online: https://www.telegraph.co.uk/education/educationnews/9950934/Michael-Gove-attacks-his-critics-as-Marxist-opponents-of-improvements-to-schools.html (accessed on 25 March 2019).

Valkanova, Yordanka. 2014. Childhood through the ages. In *An Introduction to Early Childhood Studies*, 3rd ed. Edited by Trisha Maynard and Sacha Powell. London: SAGE, pp. 22–33.

Vygotsky, Lev Semyonovich. 1978. *Mind in society: The development of higher psychological processes*. Cambridge: Harvard University Press.

© 2019 by the author. Licensee MDPI, Basel, Switzerland. This article is an open access article distributed under the terms and conditions of the Creative Commons Attribution (CC BY) license (http://creativecommons.org/licenses/by/4.0/).

Article

Child Abandonment in England, 1741–1834: The Case of the London Foundling Hospital

Claire Phillips

School of Cultural Studies and Humanities, Leeds Beckett University, Leeds LS1 3HE, UK; drclairephillips@outlook.com

Received: 5 May 2019; Accepted: 27 June 2019; Published: 29 June 2019

Abstract: The prevailing view of abandoned children in the eighteenth and nineteenth centuries comes from Dickens' Oliver Twist. Twist was born and raised in a workhouse in nineteenth-century London. However, the workhouse was not the only, or even, the main place to which children were abandoned. The London Foundling Hospital opened in 1741 and, although admission rules were often strict, between the years 1756 and 1760, any child presented to the Hospital was admitted. This article examines the ways in which children were abandoned to the Foundling Hospital and how these children were cared for in the period 1741–1834. It charts the children's journeys through the Hospital, from their initial abandonment and admission to their eventual discharge—either through death, apprenticeship, or marriage—or their continued residence at the institution. This article provides insights into the multiple experiences of childhood abandonment and details the utility of the Hospital's surviving records. It argues that children admitted to the London Foundling Hospital received life chances they would otherwise not have received. The Hospital provided nursing, clothing, medical care, both an academic and vocational education, and a living space for those unable to survive alone in adulthood.

Keywords: childhood; foundling hospital; abandonment; poverty; institutionalisation

---

1. Introduction

The prevailing view of abandoned and orphaned children in nineteenth-century London is that perpetuated by Charles Dickens with the character Oliver Twist. Yet most children considered to be orphans during this period had at least one living parent, if not two. As Jessie B. Ramey points out, 'popular literature such as Dickens has done much to promote the lingering image of fully orphaned street children and institutional managers themselves frequently employed a melodramatic narrative of desperate children in need of rescue' (Ramey 2013, p. 43). The London Foundling Hospital was one such institution. Whilst it did not accept orphans—children had to be deposited by at least one parent—the Hospital did accept abandoned children, albeit under strict conditions. Unlike the orphanages described by Ramey and others, the Foundling Hospital only allowed parents to reclaim their children upon payment for their upkeep to date. Consequently, this was a rare occurrence (Levene 2012).

This article argues that children in the Foundling Hospital were, in comparison to the popular view set out by Dickens, well treated. The Foundling Hospital aimed to provide its children with more dignity than their workhouse, or street child, counterparts—despite their lowly status. By ensuring that their early years were spent in a family environment, and that they were clothed, fed, educated, apprenticed and provided with medical care when necessary, the Foundling Hospital showed itself to be an institution that was well intentioned and efficiently run, and one that aimed to achieve a better life for its children. Whilst Dickens' creation was sold into apprenticeship at the age of nine, half-starved, and treated appallingly by a succession of adult 'carers', the presence of the Foundling Hospital demonstrates that institutions could provide a comparatively stable, safe, and nurturing environment for children raised outside the family home.

The role played by the nurses in the care of children at the Foundling Hospital was vital to the success of the Hospital in general. They provided a family environment for the first five years of a foundling's life, which often created enduring relationships between nurse and child. Scholarly understanding of the relationships between nurses and foundlings is limited by the lack of correspondence between the nurses and foundlings. However, from the few examples of nurses' letters analysed in this article, it is possible to deduce that the bonds between these women and the children they nursed were strong enough to compel them to request permanent guardianship over their charges.

The London Foundling Hospital opened its doors on 25 March 1741. The Hospital was a long time in the making, with unsuccessful petitions to open a Foundling Hospital being raised as early as 1687. England lagged behind Europe in terms of institutional care for children. Its first orphanage, Christ's Hospital, opened in 1552 and was provided solely for the fatherless children of the City of London (Manzione 1995, p. 9). Although Christ's Hospital was never set up to be a Foundling Hospital it did not turn away abandoned children, and by the eighteenth century its experiences demonstrated the need for England to follow the European lead. Several European countries had long since been caring for their abandoned children in hospitals and homes established across the continent, in cities such as Nuremburg, Paris, Amsterdam, Madrid, and Florence amongst others (Fuchs 1984; Gavitt 1990; Gerber 2012; Harrington 2009; McCants 1997; Sherwood 1988; Terpstra 2005, 2010). There were two principal barriers to the opening of a Foundling Hospital in England. First, there was a lack of desire among rate payers to supply the necessary financial support for a hospital. Second, there was a widespread belief that foundlings were illegitimate, and that the provision of a hospital for their care would promote immoral behaviour (McClure 1981, p. 9). Sea Captain Thomas Coram, outraged by the number of unaccompanied children he saw on London's streets, resolved to overcome these barriers and provide the capital's abandoned youngsters with a moral upbringing.

The London Foundling Hospital admitted thirty children on its first night. Only healthy children were admitted initially but placing thirty children together inevitably led to the spread of illness. Two of the original admissions died before they could be re-baptised a mere two days later (McClure 1981, p. 51). Between 1756 and 1760 the Hospital operated a policy of general reception, during which any child presented at the gates was admitted regardless of health. Following the end of the general reception period and 1834, the Hospital's admissions policy changed several times, but often required women to petition the Hospital and participate in a ballot. The ages, health, and legitimacy or otherwise of the children were usually at the forefront of the process that determined their success in the ballots.

After admittance, the children were regularly moved around. Foundlings were re-baptised and put out to nurse, where they remained until the age of five. Between the ages of five and around eleven, the children resided at the Foundling Hospital, and received a formal education before they were apprenticed—although some children were apprenticed at a younger age, others remained at the Hospital until they were older, and some returned to the Hospital when their apprenticeships did not work out. Alongside the education of children, the Hospital took responsibility for the children's health, both within the hospital and whilst they were out at nurse. Additionally, children with severe disabilities remained at the Foundling Hospital for life and undertook work when they were able to do so.

The Foundling Hospital fulfilled its aim to provide care for abandoned children. In some cases, such as those with disabilities, this care was for life. Certainly, the Hospital did not disavow itself of its responsibility upon apprenticeship, as when things went wrong, children were returned to the Hospital until new provision could be made. But in all cases, the foundling children were set up for a particular kind of life. They were not graduates, physicians or engineers. They were housemaids, gardeners, and sailors (Berry 2019, p. 128). They were taught to follow, rather than give, orders. Foundlings were kept 'in their place', and that place was in the lower classes of society, to fulfil roles within the economy. Despite this, some foundlings were able to use their education to allow them to be slightly more than working class, as we shall see, some were apprenticed to shop keepers specifically due to their bookkeeping abilities. The education foundlings were provided was basic but allowed them to develop skills that were not necessarily available to children outside the Hospital.

The majority of research for this article was undertaken in the Foundling Hospital Archives at the London Metropolitan Archives (LMA). Admissions and discharge registers were consulted, as were apprenticeship indentures and education records. The medical records, showing what diseases children suffered from, were also used. The Foundling Hospital records are freely available to the public at the LMA and allow family historians and genealogists to trace the lives of children institutionalised at the Hospital. Careful cross-referencing with petitions written by women who left their children, and the admissions records which record the name and number of each child accepted by the Hospital, permit researchers to trace children throughout their time at the institution. Through cross-referencing these documents, which was impossible for foundlings to do during their own lifetimes, it is often possible for researchers to identify a foundling's birth mother and to piece together the circumstances by which they came to abandon their child 'to the mercy of the world' (Levene 2012).

Fundamental to the development of this article have been the letters written by nurses and inspectors to the administrators of the Foundling Hospital. All of the correspondence generated by those working and living in Berkshire are reproduced in Clark's text *The Correspondence of the Foundling Hospital Inspectors in Berkshire, 1757–68* (Clark 1994). This work consists of an introduction by Clark, which places the letters in context, and a reproduction of all the letters in their original format. Their publication allows those unable to travel to London access to some of the original documentation of the Foundling Hospital, and in particular provides the researcher with evidence of the relationships that emerged between the nurses and their foundling children.

2. Acceptance of Children

Admission to the Foundling Hospital, unlike that for the workhouse, was subject to strict conditions when it first opened. Children had to be under the age of two months, and free of venereal disease, scrofula, leprosy and any other infectious diseases. The child had to be presented to the Hospital by his or her mother, or some other adult known to the family. The prospective foundlings and their adults were placed in the Hospital's court room, and a ballot was drawn. When an adult drew a white ball, their child underwent a medical examination. When an adult drew a black ball, they and their child were turned away—under the watchful eye of the Hospital porter to ensure the child was not abandoned on the Hospital grounds. When an adult drew a red ball, their child was placed on a reserve list, and if another child was rejected due to ill-health or a breach of the age barrier, their child would undertake the medical examination (Evans 2005a, p. 87). Children who failed the medical examination or were deemed to be above the age limit for acceptance to the Hospital were returned to their accompanying adult and dismissed (McClure 1981, p. 43).

In 1756, although only one-quarter of the institution's capacity was occupied at the time, the governors of the Foundling Hospital approved a petition to be sent to the House of Commons requesting funds to expand the charity. Approximately 150 children lived in the Hospital during the early 1750s, when the building come accommodate around 400, but more and more women were seeking assistance from the charity (McClure 1981, p. 76). The excess capacity within the Hospital was a consequence of the high rates of mortality experienced among the children whilst out at nurse and led to the adoption of the general reception policy in 1756. By the end of the first day of the General Reception period, 117 children had been admitted (Administrators 1799). Over the course of the first week, 299 children were accepted to the Hospital (McClure 1981, p. 81). The rapid increase in the number of children accepted by the charity led to the establishment of branch hospitals in Chester, Shrewsbury, and at Ackworth in Yorkshire. The General Reception period ended in 1760 after funding was withdrawn.

The General Reception period presented the Foundling Hospital with a number of problems. Wet-nurses proved difficult to acquire and when the children reached the age of five, large numbers returned to London to begin their education. In addition, the relaxation of medical rules meant that mortality rates within the London hospital, the branch hospitals, and among children out at nurse soared (McClure 1981, p. 102), whilst the admittance of children with disabilities made the provision of suitable apprenticeships increasingly difficult. Some of these children remained within the walls of the Hospital for their entire lives, as they were deemed unable to provide for themselves in the outside world (Administrators 1796).

The Foundling Hospital's admissions policy fluctuated following the period of the General Reception. By 1770, the ballot system had returned, but with some modifications. Mothers were required to submit a petition to the Hospital's secretary. If the petition passed, they were then asked to return to the Hospital with the child and to participate in the ballot. The consequences for drawing a white ball or black ball remained the same as they had been in the early 1750s. However, the red ball was no longer used (Evans 2005b, p. 127). By 1801, only illegitimate children were accepted for entry, a policy that prevented abandoned wives from giving up their children to be cared for by the state rather than the child's father (Barret-Ducrocq 1992, p. 40). During this period, a full examination of the circumstances surrounding the child's birth were undertaken by the governors. Mothers were expected to provide information about the child's father, details of the promises that had been broken, and proof that abandoning the child to the Foundling Hospital would allow them to return to a moral and respectable life (Sheetz-Nguyen 2012, p. 94). References from those who could attest to the mother's good character and her relationship with the father were obtained from employers, priests, and ministers.[1]

Although children admitted into the Foundling Hospital were provided with a new name, re-baptised, and had all traces of their former lives erased, careful records were kept in the event that families wanted to reclaim their children. Between 1741 and 1800, over 500 families attempted to reclaim a foundling. To ensure that the correct child was released to the correct family, mothers were encouraged to leave tokens—such as ribbons, fabrics, or coins—with their abandoned child. Those who sought to claim a child were expected to be able to describe or produce a duplicate of the token left at the Hospital (Clark and Bright 2015, p. 54; Evans 2005a, p. 141). Fewer tokens were left with children after the general reception period, but the identification of each child was made easier by the use of numbered records. Upon admission, each child was assigned a number, which was used on all official documents within the hospital—admissions, discharge, schooling, apprenticeship, and medical records. The number was also recorded on a disc, worn by the child at all times until they left the Hospital (Clark and Bright 2015, p. 54).

3. Foundlings at Nurse

Upon admission, the Hospital became responsible for every aspect of a foundling's life, from feeding and clothing them, through ensuring their safety whilst at nurse, to their education, apprenticeship, and departure from the institution. This section examines the ways in which foundlings were treated whilst at nurse and the relationships they developed with their nurse and her family. Alysa Levene's (2012) study of the care of children in the Foundling Hospital undertook a statistical analysis of the nurses and their families to identify the characteristics of women who became Foundling Hospital nurses. This section adds a qualitative dimension to that literature, drawing upon the written testimony document by Gillian Clark. The letters produced by the nurses and inspectors in the Berkshire region provide valuable insights into the emotional bonds that were developed in the first five years of a foundling's life, and emphasise the caring atmosphere in which abandoned children were nurtured.

Healthy children were immediately dispatched to a nurse, often within the locality of London. The Hospital's nursing network was vast, and nurses frequently cared for more than one child at a time. When the Hospital matched a nurse to a child, the former had to travel to London to collect the child and was expected to return them when they reached the age of five. Upon collection, the nurse was provided with a receipt that recorded the clothing issued to the child (after admission, the clothes a child had entered the Foundling Hospital in were destroyed, along with all other traces of their former lives), and the responsibilities assigned to both the nurse and the Hospital with regards to the child.

---

[1] Petitions admitted 1813–1825, A/FH/A/08/001/002/022–A/FH/A/08/001/002/034, Foundling Hospital, London Metropolitan Archives.

To ensure their duties were discharged, each nurse was supervised by an inspector (Levene 2012, p. 93). The letters written to the Foundling Hospital by the Berkshire inspectors have been transcribed by Gillian Clark (1994), and these documents provide a clear illustration of the multiple layers of care undertaken by the Foundling Hospital during the period under examination. When they were collected by their nurse, each child was provided with clothing that was to be returned to the Foundling Hospital once they reached the age of one. If the clothing was not returned in the same condition as it had been upon issue, the nurse was obliged to purchase replacements (Clark 1994, p. liv). Furthermore, if the child died whilst at nurse, it was the latter's responsibility to return the child's clothing to the Hospital so that it could be reissued. The letters from the inspectors indicate that this was often done promptly.[2]

However, the Foundling Hospital's duty to provide its children with new clothes as they grew was not always handled so proficiently. The letter sent by Inspector Bunce to Mr Collingwood, the Hospital's Secretary, stated that he had returned the clothing of two children—one of whom had recently died—but that he needed clothing for six children aged over one year old. Those children had grown out of the clothes provided for them by the Foundling Hospital and required replacements. Bunce was not the only inspector who requested new clothing or showed concern at the unsuitability of the young foundlings' apparel: in a letter from 1760, an unnamed inspector complained that 'most' of the children under their care were 'almost naked'.[3] As the responses to the inspectors' letters are not provided in Clark's compilation, we do not know whether or when the clothes arrived. However, it is clear that the Foundling Hospital was not always able to ensure that the children were suitably clothed, and that it devolved responsibility for clothing onto the nurses and inspectors.

The provision of medical care for the children at nurse was a further concern for the Foundling Hospital's inspectors. Whilst many children were cared for within the home, more serious conditions—including epidemic diseases such as measles, smallpox, and fevers—were the Hospital's responsibility to treat. The case of Catherine Towes, at nurse in Berkshire, provides a vivid example of the care provided by the Hospital to its foundlings. Inspectors were required to offer assistance to nurses with sick children, to issue remedies from a stock supplied by the Hospital, and to provide the nurses with financial access to a physician or apothecary. If the children could not be treated at nurse, or they required surgery and were able to travel, they were returned to the Foundling Hospital (Clark 1994, p. xlv). Catherine Towes remained at nurse when she contracted a fever. It is unclear how old she was from the surviving documents but as she was at nurse, it is safe to assume she was under the age of five. In 1759, Inspector Mrs Birch recorded that Catherine was sick and had been given magnesia and musk in order to prevent convulsions.[4] Mrs Birch took her responsibility towards the sick girl very seriously, and treated Catherine over the following year as she remained ill with an intermittent fever. By 14 April 1760, Mrs Birch recorded that Catherine had been in 'great danger' from a violent fever, but had recovered after being attended to with James' Fever Powder every six hours.[5] The use of James' Fever Powder indicates that Mrs Birch felt that a more professional—rather than domestic—approach was required in Catherine's case. Patent medicines such as James' Fever Powder became fashionable in the eighteenth century and offered standardised medicines to be provided for the sick in place of domestic remedies. The powder alleviated Catherine's fever and her condition improved but by 29 June 1761, Catherine's condition had worsened once more. Mrs Birch wrote that she was dangerously ill with a fever, which was 'occasioned by cutting teeth'.[6] On this occasion, the Hospital paid for an apothecary to treat Catherine. However, the treatment did not work and she died. Following Catherine's death, Mrs Birch wrote that 'I wish with all my heart I had been on

---

[2] J. Bunce to Collingwood, 1759, A/FH/A/6/1/12/2/62, Foundling Hospital, London Metropolitan Archives, quoted in (Clark 1994).
[3] Letter to Collingwood, 1760, A/FH/A/6/1/13/4/12, Foundling Hospital, London Metropolitan Archives, quote in (Clark 1994, p. 103).
[4] Letter from Mrs Birch, 1759, A/FH/A/6/1/13/2/36, Foundling Hospital, London Metropolitan Archives, quoted in (Clark 1994, p. 83).
[5] Letter from Mrs Birch, 1760, A/FH/A/6/1/13/2/37, Foundling Hospital, London Metropolitan Archives, quoted in (Clark 1994, p. 84).
[6] Letter from Mrs Birch, 1761, A/FH/A/6/1/14/2/12, Foundling Hospital, London Metropolitan Archives, quoted in (Clark 1994, p. 116).

the spot to have given James' Powder, having with all the children so often experienced its efficiency. She dyed of a fever, of which she was taken ill soon after I left the country'.[7]

Mrs Birch was clearly fond of the foundlings she cared for whilst they were at nurse in Berkshire, and willing to question the responses she received from the Foundling Hospital's governors. When dealing with another child who suffered from a fever, Mrs Birch wrote to the governors that 'had he been my own I should have administered James' Powder, but lest your govs. should imagine I had quacked their children to death, I am fearfull of using it'.[8] The correspondence demonstrates that, although the inspectors appeared to have great freedom to assess the behaviour and conduct of the nurses, the final decisions over medical care remained the responsibility of the Hospital. Catherine Towes was not the only child to suffer from fever whilst out at nurse, but she was the only one to be the subject of multiple letters. Mrs Birch tried several remedies to cure Catherine and whilst ultimately unsuccessful, the case demonstrated the dangers that foundlings faced whilst at nurse—as well as the lengths to which inspectors and governors were prepared to go in order to ensure their health.

The affection bonds built between inspectors and the foundlings was mirrored in the relationships formed between the children and their nurses. In a number of cases, the nurses requested, via their inspectors, to keep the children within their homes rather than send them back to the Foundling Hospital when they reached the age of five. In March 1760, Inspector T. Marsham wrote to the Hospital on behalf of Elizabeth Kenting, a nurse, to request 'that she be able to keep her foundling, John Woolaston, to raise as her own'.[9] Similarly, Inspector M. Jones wrote to the governors in 1764 on behalf of 'the woman who nurses Mary Rennard' as she wished to know whether she could keep the child 'for her life'.[10] Nurse Elizabeth Grout took the unusual step of writing to the Hospital governors herself, in a letter passed on by her inspector. Grout wrote passionately about her desire to keep the young foundling James Creed in her home. She wrote that 'he is to me as tho' he had been my own natural born son, and my love and affections to him is so great, that to part with him will be as to part with my life'.[11] Unfortunately, Clark's compilation of the primary sources does not include the institution's responses to nurses that had requested to adopt foundling children. Therefore, it is impossible from the surviving records to calculate the frequency with which nurses became the adoptive parents to children who had been abandoned to the Foundling Hospital's care. However, this does not diminish the argument pursued in this article. Clearly, loving relationships developed between nurses, their families, and the foundlings for whom they were responsible. Recently, Helen Berry has noted that foundlings who ran away from their apprenticeships sought out their nurses and has found evidence that foundlings requested to be apprenticed to their nurses many years after they had returned to the Hospital (Berry 2019, p. 114). During the early years of a foundling's life, it was their nurse and her family who provided the familial love and support the children required in their first five years (Levene 2012, p. 134). The bonds developed lasted for many years (Berry 2019, p. 115). Yet the Foundling Hospital retained both an interest in and ultimate control over the foundlings, particularly with regards to clothing, medical care, and their overall welfare. The Hospital took the final decisions when it came to the treatments administered to the children and whether or not they were permitted to remain with the nurses when they reached five years of age. In general, the surviving records demonstrate that the nurses, inspectors, and the Foundling Hospital worked together to ensure the safety, health, and comfort of the growing children, thus providing a clear contrast to the experiences of children in the early Victorian workhouse.

---

[7] Letter from Mrs Birch, 1761, A/FH/A/6/1/14/2/10, Foundling Hospital, London Metropolitan Archives, quoted in (Clark 1994, p. 117).
[8] Letter from Mrs Birch, 1760, A/FH/A/6/1/13/2/34, Foundling Hospital, London Metropolitan Archives, quoted in (Clark 1994, p. 82).
[9] T. Marsham to Collingwood, 1760, A/FH/A/6/1/13/13/59, Foundling Hospital, London Metropolitan Archives, quoted in (Clark 1994, pp. 107–8).
[10] Letter from M. Jones, 1764, A/FH/A/6/1/17/9/43, Foundling Hospital, London Metropolitan Archives, quoted in (Clark 1994, p. 187).
[11] Nurse Grout to the Governors, 1763, A/FH/A/6/1/16/7/5, Foundling Hospital, London Metropolitan Archives, quoted in (Clark 1994, pp. 164–65).

4. Education and Apprenticeship

At the age of five, children were returned to the London Hospital to begin their education (see the following for an extensive analysis of education in the Foundling Hospital: Rennie 2018; McClure 1981; Berry 2019). The foundlings were placed in a dormitory with other children and began their schooling and work immediately. Their education was basic but more comprehensive than that received by many of their contemporaries, who either received no education or were part of other schooling movements. By 1799, the Hospital's rules and regulations state that the children learned to read, write, and undertake accounting duties (Administrators 1799).

The foundlings followed a strict timetable throughout their time at the Hospital, and their education occupied a prominent place within it. The children rose at six o'clock during the summer months and at daybreak in the winter. The boys began the day by working the pump to ensure a sufficient water supply to the Hospital, whilst the older girls assisted the younger children to rise and dress. At half-past seven, the children had breakfast and the school day began an hour later. The boys remained in lessons until midday, whilst the girls remained in the classroom a little longer. Following lunch, the children returned to their lessons, which lasted from two until five p.m. in the summer and until dusk in the winter. Supper was served at six p.m. and the children retired to bed at eight p.m. On Saturdays, the children had half a day of lessons (Administrators 1799).

More information on the education provided to the boys at the Foundling Hospital has survived—perhaps as it was thought more appropriate for boys to receive a thorough education than girls. By 1800, the school master recorded the number of hours of reading, writing, and arithmetic undertaken by the children each day, and the surviving documents make clear that the girls received the same instruction as the boys at this time (Rennie 2018). Religion was a central component of the children's education, and religious texts formed a large part of their reading assignments (McClure 1981, p. 228). The moral aspect of a religious education was not lost on the Hospital's governors, who ensured the children attended church every Sunday.

Alongside their academic work, the children received vocational training in the hopes of providing them with experience of the likely jobs to which they would be apprenticed. The boys undertook work in the gardens, assisted the servants, worked the water pump, and cleaned the courtyard and chapel (Administrators 1799). Whilst the boys undertook physical work, the girls were taught to sew, an activity that assisted the Foundling Hospital's fundraising activities. The Administrators noted that 'the annual average produce of the girls [in sewing] is 12*l* each, from eleven to fourteen years of age; and that of the little girls, aged seven to eleven is 2*l*.13*s* for each' (Administrators 1799). The schoolmaster reported in March 1819 that the girls of the Hospital had made six night dresses, one dozen aprons, half a dozen boys' shirts, two dozen pin cloths, one dozen caps, and one dozen pocket handkerchiefs.[12] Whilst there is no mention in the documents of boys having undertaken work to be sold, little boys were recorded as having darned the socks of other foundlings (Administrators 1799). The vocational work done by the foundlings was considered a crucial part of their education, as whilst reading, writing, and arithmetic were important, the Hospital accepted that most foundlings were likely to find apprenticeships in more physically demanding roles—particularly domestic service for girls, and gardening and cleaning for boys. However, many boys were apprenticed to shopkeepers also, a profession for which an ability to keep accounts was clearly beneficial.

Even after they embarked upon their apprenticeships, the foundlings remained under the watchful eye of the Foundling Hospital. Both the matron and the schoolmaster made regular visits to foundlings whilst they were on apprenticeships, and children were returned to the Hospital if an apprenticeship was deemed unsuitable or the child had run away. These children remained within the walls of the Hospital until a suitable alternative could be found. Many of the girls, like Martha Maria Clayton, went into domestic service. At fourteen, Martha was apprenticed to Carr Ellion Lucas, a surgeon. As a

---

[12] Weekly Reports, 1819, A/FH/A/23/001/001, Foundling Hospital, London Metropolitan Archives.

girl, it is unlikely Clayton was apprenticed to do anything other than domestic service.[13] Yet Diane Boycott, also fourteen, was apprenticed to a schoolmistress named Ann Herr. It is possible that Diane was apprenticed as a domestic servant, but it is also conceivable that she was apprenticed as a teacher because of the education she had received at the Foundling Hospital.[14] Her apprenticeship indenture does not provide evidence of the work that she was required to undertake as her apprenticeship.

Not all foundlings could be apprenticed out from the Hospital, however. Disabled children in particular were liable to be found unsuitable for apprenticeships. The 1796 *Account of the Foundling Hospital* stated that not all children could be apprenticed, due to the large number of children accepted during the general reception. Those of 'imbecility of body, or mind,' were expected to 'remain at the Hospital, as comfortable and useful as their capacities will allow' (Administrators 1796). Some allowances were made for children with particular disabilities. Those who were blind were occasionally taught music, at the Hospital's expense, which allowed them to make money and live a relatively comfortable life outside the Hospital. The 1796 *Account* indicates that the governors were first encouraged to teach a blind child music in 1758 and, by 1796, three children were successfully living independent of the Hospital by earning a living through music (Administrators 1796).

5. Medical Care

Of course, children were not only sick whilst out at nurse—they regularly became ill within the walls of the Foundling Hospital itself. The medical care provided to children in the Foundling Hospital has been analysed by Alysa Levene (2012), Ashley Mathisen (2013), Claire Rennie (2016), and to an extent by Ruth McClure (1981). However, due to the surfeit of primary source material available with regards to the health of foundlings, there has been little overlap in discussions of child health in the London Foundling Hospital. This section discusses the illnesses children suffered from within the Hospital and draws tentative conclusions about the treatment they received.

Although all children were examined to confirm their health upon entry (except for during the period of the General Reception), when oftentimes weak and malnourished children from a variety of backgrounds were placed together, infectious diseases spread like wildfire. Therefore, the provision of sound medical care was an important focus for the Foundling Hospital. Instances of common conditions, such as coughs, colds, sore throats and sore ears, were listed with regularity within the records of the Hospital infirmaries and were accompanied by frequent mentions of other conditions. Skin conditions, particularly the itch, scrofula, and scald head, were prominent features at the London hospital and the provincial branches—and were regularly noted in letters to the hospital from inspectors. In June 1823, Rebecca Collier was admitted to the London hospital infirmary with scrofula.[15] She remained in the Hospital infirmary for over a year before being discharged, demonstrating that her condition was difficult to treat.

Physicians and apothecaries were employed by the Foundling Hospital to provide specialist care for children who suffered from a range of conditions. The surviving records illustrate the range of conditions typically present within the hospital and highlight outbreaks of epidemic diseases such as measles, smallpox, and whooping cough. However, there are few examples that provide evidence of precisely how sick children were treated. With the exception of Buchan's *Domestic Medicine* (Buchan 1781), written by the Ackworth branch's attending physician, and the records of the medical experiments undertaken on foundling children by William Watson and Robert McClellan (for smallpox inoculations and the treatment of skin conditions respectively), the treatment administered to children within the Foundling Hospital remains a mystery. Although Buchan, William Cadogan and others administered medical care to the children of the Foundling Hospital and wrote texts on the care of

---

[13] Apprenticeship Indentures, 1806–1807, A/FH/A/12/004/097/001, Foundling Hospital, London Metropolitan Archives.
[14] Apprenticeship Indentures, 1816–1817, A/FH/A/12/004/122, Foundling Hospital, London Metropolitan Archives.
[15] Weekly Reports on the Sick, June 1823, A/FH/A/18/005/010, Foundling Hospital, London Metropolitan Archives.

children, it is impossible to state with certainty that their books detailed the medical care that the children actually received. As can be seen in their texts, and domestic receipt books used within homes during the eighteenth century, numerous remedies existed for the treatment of common illnesses (Rennie 2016). The surviving evidence does not permit us to say with certainty whether the nurses who provided day-to-day care within the Hospital drew upon their knowledge of domestic receipt books to administer forms of treatment to sick children in their care. The London Foundling Hospital did not provide treatment for all its children. Alongside the Hospital's onsite infirmary, two other locations offered medical care to the foundlings—the Brill at St Pancras and Battle Bridge. The available sources for both of these sites do not provide sufficient information to identify whether specialist care was undertaken at particular sites, nor is there any suggestion that the two external locations were used only when the Hospital infirmary could not accommodate the sick. The Battle Bridge records demonstrate that the children who were sent there were not suffering from life threatening conditions. Instead, the patients at Battle Bridge—with one notable exception—suffered from regular childhood illnesses. In the exceptional case, between 2 March and 1 May 1759 eighteen children were admitted to Battle Bridge with 'sore bottom'. Some of the children also suffered ailments such as 'sick', 'sore legs', and sore neck.[16] The specific diagnosis for 'sore bottom' is unclear—it may have been a stomach bug, diarrhoea, or worms, given that so many children suffered from it over a two-month period. However, due to the limitations of the available records we do not know how 'sore bottom' or other conditions were treated at Battle Bridge. All we can deduce is that the Hospital authorities recognised the need to move sick children to a specific site at which some form of medical care could be undertaken.

Yet the regularity with which infectious diseases appeared in the Hospital infirmary records suggests that infectious children were not moved out of the Hospital with sufficient speed. In August 1823, twenty-three children were listed as suffering from measles—a significant spike in cases.[17] During the autumn months, whooping cough replaced measles, with outbreaks recorded on 26 September (fifteen children) and 17 October (nineteen children).[18] The incidence of smallpox within the records for the nineteenth century are comparatively low, as during the late-eighteenth century, foundlings were inoculated against the disease when they returned from nurse (if they had already had the disease, they were not inoculated, as survival provided immunity).[19] The inoculation process was long, expensive and complicated, and required the patient to follow a strict regimen prior to, during, and after the inoculation took place. However, the consequences of a smallpox outbreak in the Hospital were severe enough to compel the governors to foot the bill. By 1809, there is evidence to suggest that the Foundling Hospital had moved from inoculation to vaccination against smallpox. The *Instructions Respecting Vaccination*, dated to 1809, indicate that no health regimen was required before, during or after the vaccination. Therefore, the procedure was cheaper, quicker and easier than inoculation, and it was taken up by the Foundling Hospital as a preventative measure.[20]

In addition to the general medical care provided within the Foundling Hospital, its branch hospitals, and two local infirmaries, two individuals had a significant impact upon the health of foundlings. The apothecary Robert McClellan used Powis Wells Water in an attempt to find a cure for children with skin conditions, whilst physician William Watson experimented on the foundlings using a smallpox inoculation. McClellan's experiments were neither invasive nor dangerous, he simply gave the foundlings spring water (Mathisen 2013, p. 32). However, Watson's experiments with smallpox inoculation proved more controversial. As the children lacked a parent to advocate on their behalf, Watson's trials—along with those undertaken by George Armstrong, physician at the London

---

[16] Weekly List of the Sick at The Brill, 1759, A/FH/A/18/004/002, Foundling Hospital, London Metropolitan Archives.
[17] Weekly Reports on the Sick, August 1823, A/FH/A/18/005/010, Foundling Hospital, London Metropolitan Archives.
[18] Weekly Reports on the Sick, September and October 1823, A/FH/A/18/005/010, Foundling Hospital, London Metropolitan Archives.
[19] Secretary's Papers, 1759–1773, A/FH/Q/1/16/002, Foundling Hospital, London Metropolitan Archives.
[20] Instructions Respecting Vaccination, Published by the National Vaccine Establishment, 1809, A/FH/A/18/010/004, Foundling Hospital, London Metropolitan Archives.

Dispensary for the Infant Poor—received criticism for using vulnerable children as 'guinea pigs', as many Foundling Hospital's across Europe did (Sherwood 1988, p. 155). Yet by providing access to children's bodies for the study of children's diseases, institutions such as the Foundling Hospital and the Dispensary for the Infant Poor provided the building blocks for the development of paediatrics in the nineteenth and twentieth centuries.

6. Conclusions

When the Foundling Hospital admitted an abandoned child, it vowed to provide the necessary care and education to nurture that child into a productive, moral member of British society. It provided the foundlings with life chances hitherto denied to abandoned children in England and, although sparse, their lives were a far cry from the image portrayed in the pages of Dickens' novels. The Foundling Hospital acquired a whole range of responsibilities to its children—the provision of a nurse and a stable family environment, clothing, education and apprenticeship, and medical care—and the institution took those responsibilities seriously. Through a combination of religious instruction, academic study, and vocational training, foundlings were presented with opportunities to enter domestic service, a variety of trades, or the armed forces. The children fortunate enough to be admitted to the hospital escaped from a life on the streets, in the workhouse, or worse, and were prepared for a life beyond the Hospital walls.

The Foundling Hospital was arguably the first children's institution to care for abandoned children in England. To those raised with an image of abandoned children influenced heavily by the cast of characters drawn by Charles Dickens, the Foundling Hospital's approach demonstrates a high degree of empathy for its charges. As this article has demonstrated, the Foundling Hospital—whilst by no means perfect—was established with good intentions when it came to the nurture and care of London's abandoned children. The relationships fostered between foundling children and their nurses comprises an important aspect of that care. The Hospital set itself up to be a parent to abandoned children and, to do so, they provided a family for foundlings—for the first five years of their lives at least. The letters written by nurses who wished to maintain responsibility for the care of their foundlings illustrates that the Hospital employed women capable of developing loving and nurturing environments during a period understood as critical to child development.

The care of abandoned children has come a long way since the opening of the Foundling Hospital in 1741. Institutions dedicated to the care of abandoned children that opened later in the nineteenth century—and into the twentieth—recognised the importance of home life throughout children's upbringing and began to foster children out for the duration of their childhood rather than just during infancy. Those who could not be boarded with families often lived in cottage or scattered homes, which were set up by a domestic family (Cottam 2017, p. 175). Yet the Foundling Hospital remained a constant presence in the lives of its children, including into adulthood. Its legacy survives to the present day in the form of the Coram charity, which still puts the welfare of abandoned and orphaned children at the core of its ethos.

Funding: This research received no external funding.

Acknowledgments: I would like to thank Pam Jarvis and Christopher Phillips for their comments on an earlier drafts of this work.

Conflicts of Interest: The author declares no conflict of interest.

References

Administrators. 1796. *An Account of the Foundling Hospital in London, for the Maintenance and Education of Exposed and Deserted Young Children*. London: Printed for the Foundling Hospital by Thomas Jones, Clifford's-Inn-Gate, Fetter Lane.

Administrators. 1799. *An Account of the Foundling Hospital in London, for the Maintenance and Education of Exposed and Deserted Young Children*, 2nd ed. London: Printed for the Foundling Hospital by Thomas Jones, Clifford's-Inn-Gate, Fetter Lane.

Barret-Ducrocq, Françoise. 1992. *Love in the Time of Victoria: Sexuality and Desire among Working-Class Men and Women in Nineteenth-Century London*. Translated by John Howe. London: Penguin.

Berry, Helen. 2019. *Orphans of Empire: The Fate of London's Foundlings*. Oxford: Oxford University Press.

Buchan, William. 1781. *Domestic Medicine: Or, a Treatise on the Prevention and Cure of Diseases by Regimen and Simple Medicines*, 7th ed. London: D. Graisberry.

Clark, Gillian. 1994. *Correspondence of the Foundling Hospital Inspectors in Berkshire, 1757–68*. Reading: Berkshire Record Society.

Clark, Gillian, and Janette Bright. 2015. The Foundling Hospital and Its Token System. *Family & Community History* 18: 53–68.

Cottam, Susan. 2017. Small and Scattered: Poor Law Children's Homes in Leeds, 1900–1950. *Family & Community History* 20: 175–92.

Evans, Tanya. 2005a. *Unfortunate Objects: Lone Mothers in Eighteenth-Century London*. Basingstoke: Palgrave Macmillan.

Evans, Tanya. 2005b. 'Unfortunate Objects': London's Unmarried Mothers in the Eighteenth Century. *Gender & History* 17: 127–53.

Fuchs, Rachel. 1984. *Abandoned Children: Foundlings and Child Welfare in Nineteenth-Century France*. Albany: State University of New York Press.

Gavitt, Philip. 1990. *Charity and Children in Renaissance Florence: The Ospedale Degli Innocenti, 1410–1536*. Ann Arbor: University of Michigan Press.

Gerber, Matthew. 2012. *Bastards: Politics, Family, and Law in Early Modern France*. Oxford: Oxford University Press.

Harrington, Joel F. 2009. *The Unwanted Child: The Fate of Foundlings, Orphans, and Juvenile Criminals in Early Modern Germany*. Chicago: University of Chicago Press.

Levene, Alysa. 2012. *Childcare, Health and Mortality at the London Foundling Hospital, 1741–1800: "Left to the Mercy of the World"*. Manchester: Manchester University Press.

Manzione, Carol Kazmierczak. 1995. *Christ's Hospital of London, 1552–1598 "A Passing Deed of Pity"*. London: Associated University Presses.

Mathisen, Ashley. 2013. Mineral Waters, Electricity and Hemlock: Devising Therapeutics for Children in Eighteenth-Century Institutions. *Medical History* 57: 28–44. [CrossRef] [PubMed]

McCants, Anne. 1997. *Civic Charity in a Golden Age: Orphan Care in Early Modern Amsterdam*. Champaign: University of Illinois Press.

McClure, Ruth K. 1981. *Coram's Children: The London Foundling Hospital in the Eighteenth Century*. New Haven: Yale University Press.

Ramey, Jessie B. 2013. *Childcare in Black and White: Working Parents and the History of Orphanages*. Urbana: University of Chicago Press.

Rennie, Claire. 2016. The Care of Sick Children in Eighteenth-Century England. Ph.D. Thesis, University of Leeds, Leeds, UK.

Rennie, Claire. 2018. The Education of Children in London's Foundling Hospital, c. 1800–1825. *Childhood in the Past* 11: 8–20. [CrossRef]

Sheetz-Nguyen, Jessica. 2012. *Victorian Women, Unwed Mothers and the London Foundling Hospital*. London: Continuum.

Sherwood, Joan. 1988. *Poverty in Eighteenth-Century Spain: The Women and Children of the Inclusa*. London: University of Toronto Press.

Terpstra, Nicholas. 2005. *Abandoned Children of the Italian Renaissance: Orphan Care in Florence and Bologna*. Baltimore: Johns Hopkins University Press.

Terpstra, Nicholas. 2010. *Lost Girls: Sex and Death in Renaissance Florence*. Baltimore: Johns Hopkins University Press.

© 2019 by the author. Licensee MDPI, Basel, Switzerland. This article is an open access article distributed under the terms and conditions of the Creative Commons Attribution (CC BY) license (http://creativecommons.org/licenses/by/4.0/).

MDPI
St. Alban-Anlage 66
4052 Basel
Switzerland
Tel. +41 61 683 77 34
Fax +41 61 302 89 18
www.mdpi.com

Genealogy Editorial Office
E-mail: genealogy@mdpi.com
www.mdpi.com/journal/genealogy

www.ingramcontent.com/pod-product-compliance
Lightning Source LLC
Chambersburg PA
CBHW040225040426
42333CB00052B/3374